Air War O
Khalkhin Gol

The Nomonhan Incident

Vladimir R. Kotelnikov

SAM PUBLICATIONS

Air Wars 2
Air War Over Khalkhin Gol: The Nomonhan Incident
by Vladimir R. Kotelnikov

First produced in 2010 by SAM Limited, under licence from SAM Publications
Media House, 21 Kingsway, Bedford, MK42 9BJ, United Kingdom

ISBN 978-1-906959-23-4

Typeset – by SAM Publications, Media House, 21 Kingsway, Bedford, MK42 9BJ, United Kingdom
Series Editor – Andy Evans
Translated from the Russian – by Gennady Sloutskiy
Designed – by Simon Sugarhood
Printed and bound in the United Kingdom – by Buxton Press

Contents

Chapter 1
A Troublesome Border

Historically, the boundary between Outer Mongolia and China has never been an easy subject to deal with and the uncertain nature of the actual border has led to many mutual territorial claims. At first, China's Northern Provinces' Authorities claimed their right for near-border Mongolian lands and after the Japanese occupation of Manchuria and the establishment of the Manchukuo puppet state it was Japan's turn to claim her territorial rights to the land. In particular, the Japanese stated their ownership of the right-bank area at 'Khalkhin Gol River', and for the proposes of this book we will omit the term 'River', because it is implied by the Mongolian word 'Gol'. The Japanese supported their claims with 19th century geographical maps drawing the borderline along the river, the Mongolians, however, drew their claimed borderline 10 to 20 kilometres further eastwards and implied the Japanese maps were faked. Later, Soviet historians would consistently state that the true reason for the Japanese territorial claims was Tokyo's desire to move the boundary further away from the constructed Solun – Halun Arshan – Hailar railway, which was of a high strategic military importance and when the military conflict began, this railway was already partially operational.

To the West of the Khalkhin Gol were the table-flat heathlands, and at Hamar Dabaa, the Khalkhin Gol's flow turns to the North, and 15 to 20 kilometres further on the river turns to the West into Lake Buir and is surrounded by desert plains. Here and there, villages and road junctions were assaulted from time to time and such hit-and-run raids were undertaken by Manchurian Army units, and Japanese participation was scarce. However, their armament was entirely of Japanese origin, and any operational planning was undertaken by the Japanese Kwantung Army Headquarters. The Mongolians, however, also enjoyed a powerful stance and in fact, the ruling regime was backed up by the Soviet Union and strongly tied to it in political, economic and military affairs. While the Mongolian armed forces were rather weak, the national government strongly relied upon the effective mutual assistance treaty with the USSR

and in fact, by the end of the 1920's, the Mongolian Army operated under the Soviet military advisers' command, and early in the 1930's Soviet Air Force units were deployed in Mongolia where they formed a separate composite squadron commanded by I.G. Mann (an Estonian). Initially, the squadron was composed of thirty-one aircraft spread over three sections: I-5 fighters, R-5 light bombers, and R-5Sh

🎧 A typical Mongolian landscape: the larger settlements were scarce.

(LSh-5) ground attack aircraft. The latter was the same R-5 modification but with four additional machine guns instead of heavy bomb racks. The squadron's personnel arrived in Mongolia from different Soviet air units on rotation, and supported the Mongolian aircraft during a number of border conflicts. After a number of such engagements from June through to December 1935, the light bombers and the attack aircraft were relocated further southwards. In January 1936, Soviet and Mongolian aircraft began performing regular joint barrage missions along the border, and on January 15, Manchurian troops crossed the frontier at Lake Haar where they were stopped by Mongolian troops supported from the air by fighters operating out of Matad Somon airfield.

A number of armed conflicts followed with the participation of either side's air forces. On February 3

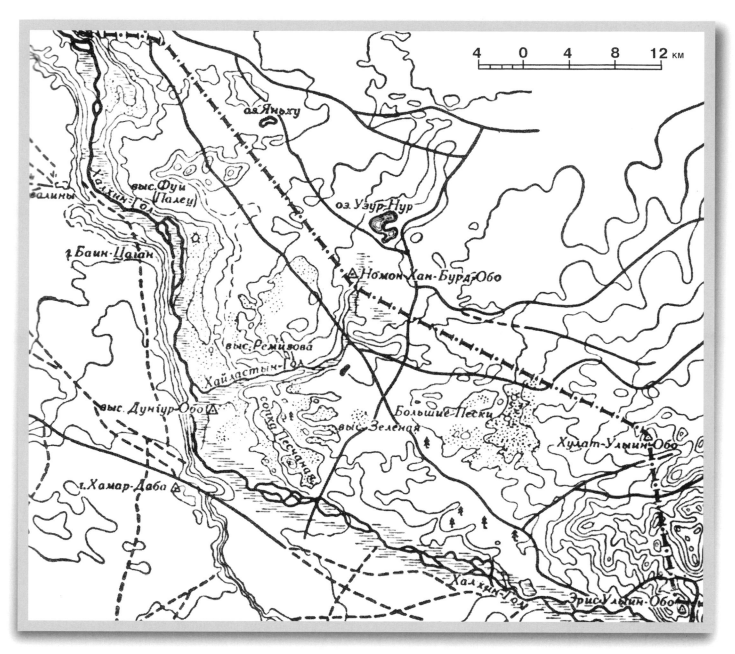

⋂ Combat operations: a Soviet map.

1936, about 600 Japanese soldiers crossed the border at Bulan Ders under the air cover of two reconnaissance aircraft. The soldiers were met by Mongolian frontier guards and the R-5 squadron from Tamtsag Bulak field, and fierce fighting broke out, and until February 12 the Japanese troops dominated, however the Mongolians forced them back, sweeping them beyond the border with R-5 bomb strikes. On March 3, an entire regiment (or just a reinforced battalion, according to Japanese sources) crossed the frontier at three points with about ninety trucks. The raid was also supported by twelve light tanks, two artillery batteries and from three to seven aircraft (depending on data sources). They were tasked with blocking the railway between Bain Tumen and Tamtsag Bulak and Lieutenant Colonel Shibuya Yasuaki commanded the operation. It didn't take long

for the Japanese detachments to occupy Assuirmiao settlement, from where they moved out to take adjacent strategic points. After that, Soviet and the Japanese sources disagree about the chronology of developments. According to Soviet sources, on March 25 an enemy platoon attacked and seized a frontier outpost in the vicinity of the Mongolryba Trust fishery at Buir Nor lake and soon after, two R-5s detected the Japanese trucks and forced them out of the outpost. Japanese sources later acknowledged the casualties resulting from that fight: one soldier dead and four wounded, and the Mongolians also took the trucks as spoils of war.

The Japanese force was opposed by a motorised infantry company, a Mongolian cavalry brigade (up to 300 horsemen), a motorised artillery battery and ten armoured vehicles. On March 31 the joint Soviet-

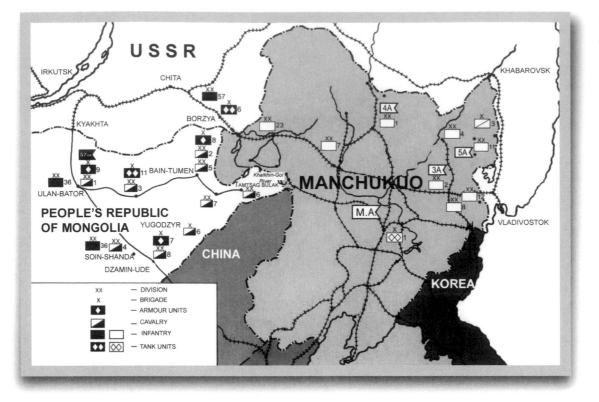

⊂ Location
of units by
May 1939.

Mongolian aviation entered the theatre of operations and carried out at least ten missions using groups of five to twelve aircraft. The R-5s took off at Baian Tumen carrying two bombs each, and having released their weapons the light bombers performed five or six strafing passes before heading home. The Mongolian pilots of Lieutenant Shagdasuren's unit were rather active on that day – for instance, the crew of aircraft 'Tactical Number 5' piloted by Demberel with Dorje as his gunner demolished an enemy truck with twenty-eight soldiers aboard and, according to Mongolian sources, shot down a Japanese reconnaissance aircraft and caused damage to another. After that, the pilot brought his aircraft home to Bain

Tumen despite it being riddled with bullet holes! Japanese sources, however, do not mention any flights on that day and the only episode they recall is a dogfight with an R-5 on April 1 when Japanese aircraft attacked Soviet armoured cars and trucks on their way to Tauran. The total losses suffered by the Kwantung Army during the incident, according to Soviet sources, amounted to 400 personnel, forty motor vehicles, eight aircraft and two tankettes. The Japanese noted that the Soviet-Mongolian air force lost three aircraft and three more were reported as damaged. As for the Soviet squadrons, two pilots were acknowledged as wounded (of which one would not recover). After the conclusion of the new treaty between Mongolia and the USSR on March 12 1936, the Soviet military presence in the region was enlarged and when Red Army regular units arrived, the 57th Special Rifle Corps was formed in September 1937.

The Start of the Conflict

Both Soviet and Japanese sources describe the various scenarios of the conflict as 'The Khalkhin Gol fights' however in the USSR it was more commonly known as 'The Nomonhan Incident'. The former states that on May 11 a unit of the Manchuria Bargut Cavalry Brigade, escorted by armoured cars attacked the Mongolian guard post to the west of Nomonhan Burd Obo Mountain and being only a small force the Mongols retreated behind the Khalkhin Gol River. However, the Japanese claim that there were no such guard posts on the right-side of the riverbank at all, and that it was Mongolian horsemen who crossed the river and attacked the Barguts, pushing them

⊍ Japanese troops advancing to the Khalkhin-Gol.

⋔ An R-5Sh attack aircraft of the 150th Regiment after an emergency landing. Note the additional machine-guns in fairings under the lower wing. The 150th Regiment was originally equipped with single-engined R-5 and R-5Sh biplanes.

⋃ I-15bis fighter from the original 1937 series.

◠ Two I-16 Type 5 fighters at an airfield in Mongolia, 1939. This type is easily distinguishable by its sliding-type canopy, fully covering the cockpit.

eastwards before they were repelled. The Soviet Union entered the fray to support Mongolia with a note of protest to Tokyo; however, this went without a response. Therefore, the problem was deemed as 'needing to be resolved at the point of a bayonet', and both parties began to reinforce their military presence in the conflict area, and this included aviation units.

Analysis of the Forces

First let's examine and compare both sides' air assets, and by far the weakest component was the Mongolian one. By the end of 1938, the MPR Air Force had thirty-nine R-5 light bombers and R-5Sh attack aircraft, and six R-5 trainers manufactured in the early 1930s at its

disposal. These obsolete biplanes were manned by twenty-seven Mongol pilots of dubious qualification! The key battle units included the 1st Ground Attack Regiment (seventeen × R-5Sh) and the 2nd Light Bomber Regiment (nineteen × R-5) at Matad airfield. As for the Soviet Air Force itself, in Mongolia it was represented by the 100th Combined Air Brigade commanded by Colonel Kalinychev and was known under the somewhat exotic designation of 'the 57th Corps' Air Force" and even 'Comrade Feklenko's Air Force' (after the Corps Commander's last name). The Brigade was composed of two regiments: the 70th Fighter Air Regiment (IAP) commanded by Major V.M. Zabaluev and the 150th High-Speed Bomber Air

↯ SB bomber after a crash landing in spring 1939. The 150th Regiment only started to master these new SB bombers from the beginning of 1939.

⌒ Ki-10 fighter, captured in China, at the NII VVS test field.

Regiment (SBAP) under Major M.F. Burmistrov's command. After the 1938 restructuring, a Soviet air regiment (five squadron's × 12 aircraft) was a considerable force. On paper, it would be composed of sixty planes, but in fact, by the middle of May the 70th IAP's stock included only fourteen I-15bis biplanes and twenty-four newer and more advanced I-16 monoplanes. The I-15bis was certainly an outdated aircraft with poor flight performance and their only merit was their firepower, as each fighter was equipped with four 7.62 mm PV-1 machine guns. As for the I-16, all those in Mongolia were of type 5 with M-25A powerplant and 2 ShKAS machine guns with a speed somewhat lower than that of a Japanese Ki-27 fighter; however, this deficiency was counterbalanced with the better 'per second' firing rate. It must be said though that these machines were badly worn, and this fact severely reduced their combat effectiveness. Anyway, by May 20, only thirteen I-16 and I-15bis fighters were fully intact and operable, and many of the pilots were too young and also lacked the appropriate training in modern combat tactics. Nevertheless the regiment was deployed at Tamtsag Bulak airfield, 100 kilometres to the West of Khalkhin Gol River.

The 150th SBAP was in a state of rearmament and had earlier been a combined regiment that included both light bomber and attack aircraft squadrons. In

⌒ Ki-27-Ko Japanese fighter.

addition it also had some outdated R-5 and R-5Sh biplanes in its stock but was now being transformed into a high-speed bombing regiment as Tupolev's twin-engine SB (high-speed bombers) were arriving from Irkutsk. Twenty-five of them were shipped to the Trans-Baikal Domna airfield unassembled, and the other fifteen were air-freighted in a 'ready-to-operate state'. By May 1, a total of thirty-six such bombers had arrived in Mongolia and another SB was transferred to the Brigade's Command. By May 27, some twenty-nine SB and seventeen R-5Sh were operational, and this rearmament process continued into conflict and was finally completed in June. A total of fifty-seven SB's eventually entered the 150th SBAP, including a number of improved 'Series 96' aircraft with three-bladed variable-pitch propellers, hydraulically-driven flaps and additional external bomb racks, and by using a shorter range to target, this aircraft type could deliver a 1,500kg bomb load. The regiment's squadrons were spread across several fields in the vicinity of Bain Tumen, about 300 km on the West of Khalkhin Gol.

The Japanese continued to insist that some reconnaissance aircraft and R-Zet light bombers also took part in the Khalkhin Gol conflict. However, this is incorrect as those aircraft types would be used later in 1938 in the course of another war action between the parties at Lake Khasan only, not at Khalkhin Gol. As for the Japanese, they had at their disposal in Manchuria the 2nd Air Division (Hikosidan) commanded by Lieutenant General T. Giga and this division comprised four brigades (Hikodan), which included two regiments (Sentai) and most of these regiments consisted of three squadrons (Chutai). Reconnaissance and bomber squadrons counted six aircraft each and a fighter squadron of ten aircraft.

Three fighter regiments were equipped with the all-metal Ki-27 monoplanes, and the fourth – with the older Ki-10 biplanes. The Ki-27 (Type 97) classified as the I-97 in Soviet reference books, was a relatively modern aircraft combining high speed and excellent manoeuvring performance. While the aircraft's aerodynamics was impaired by the non-retractable undercarriage, the same situation helped decrease the aircraft's deadweight. The Japanese designers also rejected the idea of the pilot's seat being armour plated and also limited the aircraft's weaponry to twin 7.69mm 'Type 89' machine guns, which demonstrated a somewhat lower firing rate than their Russian ShKAS counterparts. On the other hand, the Ki-27 was a little faster than I-16 Type 5 and had a superb turning radius and climbing performance, although the I-16, with its sensitive in-flight controls, tended to sway side-to-side while firing – which resulted in a

⬇ Ki-21-Otsu twin-engined bombers of the 61st Regiment.　　　⬆ Two Fiat BR.20 (Type I) bombers of the 12th Regiment.

♋ Two Ki-30 light bombers in flight.

somewhat 'scattered' fire. All Ki-27 fighters were equipped with radio receivers, and the flight commanders' aircraft contained transmitters as well, as this helped the pilots improve their combat performance through better co-ordination. However, Japanese sources complained about the poor quality and unreliability of their radio equipment. On the other hand, Soviet fighters of that period did not have any radios at all! The Ki-27 demonstrated a longer range than the Soviet fighters, and those with the 'Ki-27-Otsu' modification could carry additional outboard fuel tanks under the wing and with those mounted, the fighter's range exceeded that of the Soviet SB bomber. Instead of additional fuel tanks, light bombs could be carried under the aircraft's wing. Also, some Soviet pilots had already encountered the Ki-27 in China as the result of Soviet military assistance to Chiang Kai-shek's Army.

The Ki-10 (Type 95, or I-95 in the Soviet designation) was much more familiar to the Soviet pilots who had fought in China. A captured example of this type was delivered to the USSR and thoroughly tested at the Air Force Scientific Testing Institute (NII VVS). Its flight performance characteristics were found to be much worse than those of Soviet fighters, and the Ki-10 was thus categorised as an outdated

♋ Ki-32 light bombers.

model. The fighter's armament was the same as the Ki-27's, but the on-board radio was missing. The main Japanese bomber of that time was the Ki-30, a single-engine monoplane (Type 37, or LB-97), with 450kg bomb-carrying capacity, and a small number of the improved Ki-32 (Type 98, or LB-98) bombers were also in stock and their principal improvements included a liquid-cooled engine that had replaced the air-cooled powerplant of Ki-30 bombers. It should be noted that both types were relatively fast in flight: the Ki-30 (without bombs) would reach 432km/h speed, which was comparable with the I-16 Type 5's performance and surpassed that of the I-15bis. Another two bomber regiments were completely equipped with the modern twin-engine Ki-21 high-speed bombers (Type 97, or SB-97), and another with the Fiat BR.20 (Type I) bombers imported from Italy. Soviet sources also include some references to the SB-96 medium-class bombers (the Soviet designation for G3M/Type 96 aircraft) however; this type was employed in combat operations in China only, and never at Khalkhin Gol. The Ki-21 bomber was an up-to-date aircraft comparable with its Soviet SB counterpart; in fact it was even a little better from the perspective of its maximum speed, flight range and nominal bomb load. The Italian BR.20 was heavier than the SB, could carry more bombs and also had a longer range, and for defensive armament a single 12.7mm machine gun was carried. In May 1939 Soviet intelligence delivered the specifications of this aircraft type (in Japanese) to Moscow together with snapshots.

The long-range reconnaissance function was performed by the Ki-15 monoplane (Type 97, or R-97), a high-speed aircraft with the ceiling above the Soviet fighters' range and there were also some old Ki-4 (Type 94) biplanes available for the task. Soviet intelligence considered the Ki-4 to be a light bomber and classified it as the LB-94. Finally, the Japanese also had a limited

number of their most modern Ki-36 monoplanes available for short-range reconnaissance and light attack duties (with the bomb load limited to 150kg). Also Japanese aircrews were better trained than their Soviet counterparts and, more importantly, they had gained some practical experience during their participation in the Chinese War. On 12 May the Japanese Command ordered the establishment of a task air force known as 'Rindzi' and was to include the 24th Regiment (twenty × Ki-27) and two squadrons of the 10th Regiment (a reconnaissance squadron with six Ki-15s and bomber squadron with six Ki-30s). The 'Rindzi' was put under the command of the 24th Regiment's Lieutenant Colonel K. Matsumura and on May 13 the task force arrived at Hailar airfield, some 160km to the north from the disputed riverside, and began performing missions in the vicinity of Khalkhin Gol River.

The First Air-to-Air Actions

The Japanese asserted that the first actual 'dogfight' over the disputed area took place on May 20, when a flight of Ki-27s led by Matsumura is said to have intercepted an R-Zet protected by a pair of I-16s. The two Soviet fighters fled and the biplane was shot down. However, in Soviet documents there is no mention of either that episode or indeed of any flights

Ⓝ Ki-15 reconnaissance aircraft.

Ⓥ Ki-36 multi-purpose liaison aircraft.

◑ The Ki-4 could be used as a reconnaissance aircraft or a light bomber.

on that day, which makes the story of the lost R-Zet rather a mystery. However, both seem to agree on the actions that followed. On May 21 Japanese fighters attacked and shot down an R-5 liaison aircraft on its way to the 6th MPRA Cavalry Division (again this was misreported as an R-Zet), and this casualty is acknowledged in Soviet documents. The commander, pilot Suprun, was killed although his pilot observer Arkhipov safely parachuted down, and as such that aircraft was the first 'officially' acknowledged victim of the Khalkhin Gol campaign. The next air combat occurred on May 22 and was the first fighter-v-fighter episode. The dogfight was reported by both sides, but details differ significantly. According to the Japanese, a group of Ki-27s attacked six I-16 fighters and shot down three of them without loss, whereas the Soviets reported that three I-16 and two I-15bis fighters encountered five I-96s (which was the Soviet designation for the Mitsubishi A5M, or 'Type 96' carrier-based fighters). However, the truth is that Japanese naval fighters never fought at Khalkhin Gol; only the Army aviation was involved so therefore, the Soviet pilots in turn, must have mistaken Ki-27 fighters for the somewhat similarly shaped A5M. A single I-16 is reported to have been shot down and its pilot I. Lysenko killed in a close combat. The other four Soviet pilots turned and brought their fighters home safely.

Reinforcements Arrive at the River

Even as the first dogfights raged, reinforcements began to arrive on either side. On May 21 Major Kutsevalov

brought his 23rd Air Brigade from Trans-Baikal to the theatre and on May 23 the 22nd IAP fighters under Major Glazykin's command landed in Bain Tumen. The regiment consisted of twenty-eight I-16 Type 10 fighters (armed with four ShKAS machine guns) and thirty-six I-15bis. However, one of the I-15bis was lost en-route. The regiment's aircraft were all in quite good condition, but it was the pilots' lack of air-combat practice that mattered. A few days later, the 38th SBAP under Captain Artomonov's command arrived with fifty-nine SB bombers, and again one aircraft crashed en-route. Meanwhile, the Japanese were also reinforcing their air formations as on May 24, two squadrons of the 11th Regiment under Colonel Y. Noguchi brought in twenty Ki-27s and by May 27 the Japanese had a total of sixty-four aircraft in the vicinity of Khalkhin Gol at their disposal. However, Soviet intelligence overestimated Japanese aviation's presence reporting 180 enemy aircraft, including 126 fighters. The Red Army Air Force had 203 aircraft in Mongolia by then, however, most of those aircraft were not in a combat-ready state, and this perhaps explains why the Soviet pilots had so few combat missions. and avoided air engagements. The Japanese pilots, nevertheless, kept on reporting their victories. On May 26, the 11th Regiment's pilots, flying against eighteen I-16 fighters, claimed to have shot down nine of them for no loss and similarly, the 24th Regiment reported one I-16, one I-15bis and one R-Zet as their trophies on the same day. The most bizarre thing about those two reports is that no Soviet forces were airborne on that day!

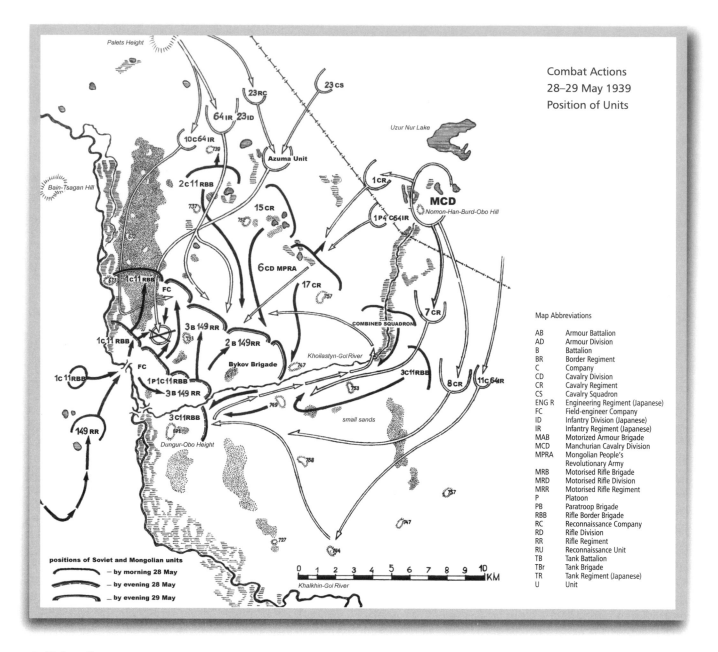

Combat Actions
28–29 May 1939
Position of Units

Map Abbreviations

AB	Armour Battalion
AD	Armour Division
B	Battalion
BR	Border Regiment
C	Company
CD	Cavalry Division
CR	Cavalry Regiment
CS	Cavalry Squadron
ENG R	Engineering Regiment (Japanese)
FC	Field-engineer Company
ID	Infantry Division (Japanese)
IR	Infantry Regiment (Japanese)
MAB	Motorized Armour Brigade
MCD	Manchurian Cavalry Division
MPRA	Mongolian People's Revolutionary Army
MRB	Motorised Rifle Brigade
MRD	Motorised Rifle Division
MRR	Motorised Rifle Regiment
P	Platoon
PB	Paratroop Brigade
RBB	Rifle Border Brigade
RC	Reconnaissance Company
RD	Rifle Division
RR	Rifle Regiment
RU	Reconnaissance Unit
TB	Tank Battalion
TBr	Tank Brigade
TR	Tank Regiment (Japanese)
U	Unit

positions of Soviet and Mongolian units
— by morning 28 May
— by evening 28 May
— by evening 29 May

A False Start

In the early morning of May 27, a squadron from 22nd IAP, commanded by Senior Lieutenant Cherenkov moved out to a landing zone close to Hamar Dabaa, and later in the day, six of their I-16 fighters went into combat with nine Ki-27s and were badly beaten up. Two Soviet fighters were shot down, and the Squadron Commander Cherenkov was killed. Another misfortune befell I-16 pilot Pyankov who was wounded but managed to bail out of his burning aircraft. The third fighter was also badly damaged and crash landed killing its pilot Savchenko, and two more fighters returned home with multiple bullet holes. The second flight of May 27 resulted in another two I-16 emergency landings due to engine failures and the Japanese reported that their pilot H. Sinohara had shot down four I-16s. The next day, three I-15bis fought with a large group of Japanese fighters above the river, where the Japanese took advantage of their numerical superiority and quickly brought down the

Soviet trio. All three Soviet pilots were killed. Later on, another I-15bis squadron took off from Tamtsag Bulak airfield to meet their fate, as eighteen Ki-27 fighters fell out of the clouds above and smashed them. Six Soviet aircraft were brought down, and a seventh force-landed and was destroyed by the Japanese. Five pilots were killed, and one escaped. Two battle-damaged I-15bis made their way to the nearest airfield, including the aircraft of the wounded Squadron Commander Balashov. The Japanese pilots' reports again exaggerated their victory on a 'heroic' scale as they claimed to have fought an overwhelming force of sixty(!) I-15bis and I-16 fighters and destroyed forty-two of them, admitting the loss of just a single Ki-27. On May 28, the 57th Corps Commander Feklenko reported to Moscow that the Japanese had total air superiority and that the Soviet fighters' were unable to protect the troops against bombing and strafing runs. Meanwhile, the high-speed SB bombers spent the first month of the conflict performing mostly long-range reconnaissance flights, as the aircraft's higher speed it less vulnerable than its R-5 predecessor, but its restricted downward visibility and lack of photographic equipment were critical features limiting the use of the aircraft. In addition, the flight personnel had only vague ideas about the enemy army's organisation and combat equipment, the latter resulting in repeated obscure phrasings in the reports, such as 'rather a lot of', 'many', 'a conglomerate of' or 'an indeterminate number of'. As late as June 16, three AFA-13 cameras were delivered from the mainland and custom-installed on reconnaissance aircraft. Later Soviet military experts would come to the conclusion that 'In the initial period of the conflict… the Air Force of the 57th Special Corps obviously suffered an ignominious defeat'.

◑ Mongolian gunners man an anti-aircraft unit equipped with a coupled Maxim machine-gun.

Moscow Makes Arrangements

In the aftermath of this debacle, Moscow undertook a number of urgent steps particularly in the area of combat experience, or the lack of, amongst Soviet pilots. As a remedy a pack of expert Soviet aviators with a proven record of warfare in Spain and China was sent to Mongolia. This taskforce was headed by the Red Army Air Force Chief Deputy, Corps Commander Y.V. Smushkevich who had recently returned from Spain and was now appointed the new Commander of the 57th Corps Air Force. On May 29 three brand new DC-3s took off from Moscow Central Airport and headed to the East. These aircraft were flown by A. Golovanov (later he would become the Long-Range Aviation General Officer-in-Command and Air Chief Marshal), M. Nyukhtikov (a famous test pilot) and V. Grachev (later he would pilot the C-47 with Joseph Stalin on board as the Soviet Leader visited Teheran in 1943). Their cabins carried forty-eight pilots, navigators and engineers, eleven of whom wore the 'Hero of the Soviet Union' star on their tunics and all were experienced in combat against Chinese aircraft. Despite a minor inconvenience right after take-off (Nuchtikov's DC-3 failed to retract the landing gear and had to fly all the way to Kazan with the wheels out), on June 2 they landed at a Trans-Baikal airbase where fully assembled and ready-to-operate fighters awaited their pilots.

In Mongolia, Smushkevich tackled the problem energetically, taking the opportunity to make the maximum use of a three-week lull on the frontier by sending new pilots on training missions. The airfields' ground facilities were also uncomplicated – felt tents (yurts) served as living quarters; fuel transporters and other vehicles were simply covered with camouflage nets, and the command post would often consist of a tent with a field telephone sitting on a drinking water barrel and a few stools around. By the end of June twenty-eight operational and fourteen reserve airfields

◑ Major Glazykin, Commander of the 22nd IAP.

were ready and each housed a maximum of fifteen aircraft. The fields were grouped close together in order to facilitate the delivery of supplies and as the pilots' skills improved, new squadrons were relocated towards the frontier. The aces that had arrived from Moscow now took leading positions in the Soviet air regiments and squadrons, and before his departure from Moscow Smushkevich promised that the newer I-16 and I-153 series fighters would be delivered as soon as possible to replace the outdated aircraft, and in fact these additional aircraft soon began to arrive from the Trans-Baikal region.

On May 29 the Red Army Air Force Chief, A.D. Loktionov, asked the Defence Commissar, K.E. Voroshilov, about the suitability of bringing in two SB squadrons from Ovruch and Shatalovo and a regiment from Krasnoyarsk. Later, it was decided to

◑ A group of pilots and engineers on their arrival from Moscow with the DC-3 transport. The first on the left is Y.V. Smushkevich, Deputy Head of the VVS RKKA Department, and the second is Colonel I. Lakeev. To the right is Military Engineer of the 1st Rank I. Prachik.

relocate only a limited number of crews from the 60th, the 18th and the 52nd SBAP and send them to reinforce the 150th SBAP without the aircraft. On June 2 Corps Commander G.K. Zhukov, the Deputy Commander of Byelorussian Military District, was summoned from Minsk to Moscow, Commissar of defence K.E. Voroshilov ordered him to the post of the 57th Corps Commander. Within a day Zhukov had left for Mongolia. In the morning of June 5 he arrived in Tamtsag Bulak and after a brief analysis of the situation, Zhukov realised that a further build-up of forces was necessary, and thereby Moscow issued an order to transform the 57th Corps into the 1st Army Group. By June 21 1939, the Soviet side had a total of 301 aircraft at its disposal in the conflict zone, including ninety-five I-16s, fifty-six I-15bis, 135 SBs and fifteen R-5Sh's. The Japanese had less than half that number – 126 aircraft, including seventy-eight Ki-27 fighters, twelve Ki-15 air reconnaissance planes, six multi-purpose Ki-36 aircraft, six Ki-30 light bombers, twelve Ki-21 bombers and twelve BR.20 bombers spread across airfields at Hailar, Chiangchunmiao and Kanchuermiao. Soviet reconnaissance reports largely overestimated the enemies' airpower and doubled it to supposedly include 260 aircraft, including 125 fighters. An interesting aspect of the Khalkhin Gol conflict was the introduction of camouflage schemes. Before the conflict the Red Army Air Force used only two colour schemes, with most aircraft painted green on top and light blue underneath. However, SB bombers, for the sake of improved speed, were coated with smooth light-grey enamel all over, and it was these bombers which first underwent the process of 'pitching' and 'blotching' with green paint. The paint was applied by either airbrush or paint brush – whatever was available. The resulting patterns were rather individual, but looked homogeneous and dull, much to the satisfaction of camouflage application instructors. Later, I-153 fighters (also originally in light grey) and DC-3 transports would likewise be disguised.

Chapter 2
The Second Phase

On June 20, Soviet troops tested the Japanese defences when an infantry battalion of the 149th Rifle Regiment, supported by armoured vehicles attacked the Soviet positions in the vicinity of Depden Sume. The assault proved to be a failure: three armoured cars were destroyed, and the infantry was forced back. Two days later, both sides seemed to have realised the need to gain superiority in the air first – and adopted the same tactics – mass fighter raids. This resulted in a large-scale air battle between the opponents' fighters. The Soviets reported some fifty-six I-16 and 49 I-15bis fighters, whereas the Japanese would later report that 120 fighters were involved from their side. The first clash occurred above Hamar Dabaa hill when a dozen I-16 and nine I-15bis of 22nd IAP were dive-attacked by a swarm of Ki-27's. Soviet sources speak of about 'thirty planes, at least', while the Japanese claim that these were just eighteen fighters of the 24th Regiment. The Japanese commenced the fight with a slashing attack upon the I-16 squadron – and immediately brought down and wounded the commander, Commander Savkin who, however, managed to 'belly-land' his fighter, and escape before the Japanese swooped in to finish off his aircraft. After that, the I-15bis became the targets. The biplanes manoeuvred heavily to take advantage of their shorter turning radius; nevertheless the Japanese knocked down three of them and proceeded to destroy any force-landed fighters. Surprisingly, all three Soviet pilots survived. At that point, an I-16 fighter squadron of the 70th IAP came to the rescue and repelled the Japanese. The second mass dogfight of that day took place a few hours later near Bain Tsagan hill. The Japanese claimed twenty-five Soviet aircraft destroyed while the Russians acknowledged the loss of ten I-15bis and three I-16 fighters and eleven pilots, including the 22nd IAP commander Major Glazykin (after this, a veteran of the Spanish campaign, G. Kravchenko, took over command). Later, fourteen crashed fighters were found on the Mongolia steppes

⊍ Red Army soldiers passing by the debris of a Ki-27 fighter from the 11th Regiment's 3rd Squadron.

◑ I-16 Type 10 fighter of the 70th IAP at Tamtsag Bulak airfield, July 1939. The red stars on the fuselage sides and on the wing upper surfaces were painted over with camouflage.

◔ The command post of the 1st Army Group Air Force at Khamar Daba mountain.

○ I-16 fighters of the 70th IAP at an airfield in Mongolia.

and eleven were reported by reconnaissance from the Manchurian side of the frontier. However, it was difficult to distinguish the crashed Japanese planes from the Soviet ones.

Later in the day, the SB bombers performed their first sweeping raid over the Japanese positions and returned home without any losses and having 'licked wounds', both sides resumed mass air dogfights on June 24. At first, eight I-16 and nine I-15bis clashed with about twenty Ki-27 fighters; soon eight more I-16 joined the dogfight. The numerical advantage resulted (according to the Soviet reports) in seven Japanese fighters being shot down. The 70th IAP lost two I-15bis; one of them was finished off by the Japanese on the ground immediately after a forced landing. Later in the day, some fifty-four Soviet fighters clashed with two Japanese groups of twenty aircraft each and the Soviet side reported nine enemy fighters shot down without loss, however a Japanese pilot killed himself after parachuting right into a group of Red Army infantrymen. The Japanese reports, on the contrary, suggest that the Soviets lost seventeen fighters and the Japanese only two (including the pilots). Another landmark of June 24 was the first Japanese fighter attack on Soviet bombers. Twenty-three SBs were intercepted by Ki-27s on their way back from a raid on the Khalkhin Gol east bank. As a result, the 150th SBAP reported one radio-operator gunner wounded after having shot down an enemy aircraft. After a one-day bad weather break, on June 26 dogfights resumed and in the afternoon Japanese fighters appeared in the skies above the Buir Nor lake

in the vicinity of the Mongolryba fisheries. They were met by twenty-seven I-16 and thirteen I-15bis fighters lead by the 70th IAP commander Major V.M. Zabaluev. They reported that a force of Ki-27s had 'declined the dogfight' and seemingly fled towards Chiangchunmiao. Having decided that this retreat was a sign of fear, the Soviet aces began a pursuit that led them into a deliberate trap. On the way back to Chiangchunmiao the Soviet group was suddenly ambushed by forty Japanese fighters. The situation was saved by Colonel A.I. Gusev's intuition, when from his advanced command point at Hamar Dabaa hill he felt something was wrong and sent the 22nd

◑ Ki-27 fighters of the 64th Regiment at an airfield in Manchukuo.

⟳ Soviet 7th Motorised Armour Brigade commanders observing an air combat engagement

☊ Colonel A. Gusev (to the left) and the new commander of the 22nd IAP Major G. Kravchenko.

☊ Fighter pilots in front of an I-16.

IAP's twenty I-16s and twenty-one I-15bis under Major G. Kravchenko's command to the Zabaluev's mission's rescue. This assistance arrived just in time as Zabaluev's fighters were already short of ammunition, and the commander himself had made a forced landing on the enemy side. Captain S. Gritsevets landed his I-16 and helped cram Major V.M. Zabaluev into the small cockpit and took off again, thus stealing him from under the noses of approaching horsed Barguts (Manchurian Mongols). The 1.5-hour long air battle resulted in the loss of three Soviet I-16 and one I-15bis fighters. Pilot Gaidobrus collided in the air with a Japanese fighter but managed to cross the front line; crash landed, and survived the accident with a few bruises. The 70th IAP pilot Aleksandrov also landed his damaged aircraft in the steppe a few dozen kilometres away from the combat area. He was sure that he had reached Mongolia but in fact, he had landed on the Manchurian side. Next day Mongolian horsemen from a reconnaissance patrol evacuated the pilot and towed away the aircraft! Once

more Soviet and Japanese documents offer strikingly different appraisals of the combat outcome. The Japanese claimed to have destroyed sixteen Soviet aircraft, and Russians reported ten Japanese shot down. As for own losses, the Japanese side would not acknowledge any, while the Soviet sources report the loss of three I-16s and one I-15bis aircraft.

Japanese Bomb Strikes

Having understood the futility of 'fighters-only' mass raids to gain air supremacy, the Japanese Command decided to bomb the enemy's airfields. At dawn on June 27 Japanese bombers took off and headed eastward. Nine Ki-30, nine Ki-21 and twelve Fiat bombers, escorted by seventy-four fighters led by Lieutenant General T. Giga divided into two task groups on reaching Mongolia. A Ki-15 reconnaissance aircraft was spotted above the 22nd IAP Tamtsag Bulak base and quickly brought down and soon observation posts began reporting a large enemy aircraft formation approaching. The alert was

◑ Soviet pilots listening to a pre-sortie briefing.

◑ Soviet pilots A. Murmylov, I. Sakharov and P. Mityagin by a I-16 Type 10 fighter.

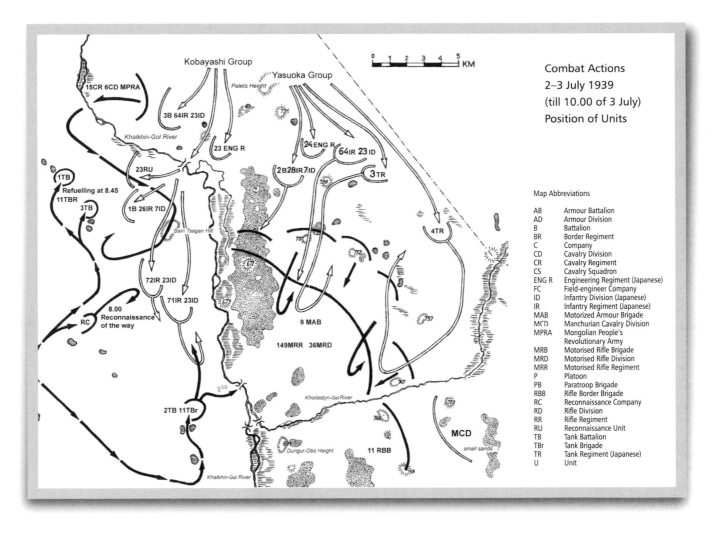

Combat Actions
2–3 July 1939
(till 10.00 of 3 July)
Position of Units

Map Abbreviations

AB	Armour Battalion
AD	Armour Division
B	Battalion
BR	Border Regiment
C	Company
CD	Cavalry Division
CR	Cavalry Regiment
CS	Cavalry Squadron
ENG R	Engineering Regiment (Japanese)
FC	Field-engineer Company
ID	Infantry Division (Japanese)
IR	Infantry Regiment (Japanese)
MAB	Motorized Armour Brigade
MCD	Manchurian Cavalry Division
MPRA	Mongolian People's Revolutionary Army
MRB	Motorised Rifle Brigade
MRD	Motorised Rifle Division
MRR	Motorised Rifle Regiment
P	Platoon
PB	Paratroop Brigade
RBB	Rifle Border Brigade
RC	Reconnaissance Company
RD	Rifle Division
RR	Rifle Regiment
RU	Reconnaissance Unit
TB	Tank Battalion
TBr	Tank Brigade
TR	Tank Regiment (Japanese)
U	Unit

signalled immediately and about ten minutes later, the bombing began with the Japanese releasing their bombs from 3,500 to 4,000m having to make their way through the anti-aircraft barrier. Meanwhile, some Soviet fighters had already taken off, while others hurriedly taxied to follow them thus the Japanese bombing failed to meet its objectives. Thirty-four I-16 and 13 I-15bis fighters entered a short clash with the Japanese escort that was seemingly reluctant to fight and soon disengaged to follow the retreating bombers. The Soviets did not give chase but reported five enemy aircraft as shot down, including two bombers. Major Kravchenko reported 'an R-97 shot down after pursuit' (which implied a Ki-15 in Soviet terms) but must have mistaken it for a similarly shaped Ki-30. The Japanese reported two Ki-27 and one Ki-30 fighters as lost and acknowledged a single Ki-21 making a forced landing in the Mongolian territory. The crew set the aircraft on fire before leaving aboard a similar bomber that landed nearby to collect them. Meanwhile, the other group of Japanese bombers performed a raid on Bain Burdu Nor airfield where the 70th IAP was deployed. Here the Japanese managed to take the enemy by surprise as Japanese saboteurs had cut the telephone lines between Russian observation posts and the regiment headquarters, and the Soviet fighters were caught on the ground. As a result, two I-16 fighters

were destroyed by direct bomb strikes, and a dozen fighters were shot down at take-off. The total losses amounted to nine I-16s and five I-15bis, and the human casualties included seven pilots killed and five wounded. The Japanese left the field unbeaten to celebrate their success.

On the same day, the Japanese bombed Bain Tumen, where SB bombers and an escort fighter squadron were deployed. Five Ki-30 and twenty-one Ki-27 bombers participated and casualties were limited to an I-15bis fighter shot down in a dogfight with Ki-27s. Ground losses included one technician killed and nineteen wounded. Japanese propaganda again exaggerated the day's success to a bizarre extent, claiming some forty-nine Soviet aircraft destroyed on the ground and ninety-nine in the air! Pilot H. Sinohara alone boasted eleven Russian fighters! The actual losses amounted to just twenty aircraft. Tokyo, however, 'honoured' the architect of the mass raids General Giga with a punitive reprimand – not for the 'bomb strikes' ineffectiveness, but for the excessive force as the Japanese General Staff was haunted by the prospect of this 'local conflict' evolving into a full-scale war, for which Japan was not yet prepared. While this was all happening the two countries maintained diplomatic relations and kept on exchanging protest notes pertaining to any minor incident. The concern

⋒ Two Ki-27 fighters in flight.

for the Japanese was that their mass raids on Mongolia could provoke the USSR to perform counterstrikes on targets in Korea and even Japan. As it turned out the Soviet Command had prepared plans for air raids against Japan, Korea and Manchukuo with dozens of military, industrial and transport targets pin-pointed. For instance, a route map was ready for a night raid on Tokyo to be carried out by two TB-3 heavy bomber regiments (up to 100 aircraft) and plans were also in place for heavy bombers to sweep along the Chinese Eastern Railway from Khabarovsk to a Trans-Baikal airbase and back. Two squadrons of the newest DB-3 long-range bombers had been already relocated to advanced positions along the Soviet bank of the Amur River. With the beginning of Khalkhin Gol combat operations, the Soviet Air Force regiments located along the South-eastern Pacific coast were placed in operational readiness, and their commanders received sealed envelopes with advance orders about the bombing targets. But the order to attack never came.

Transport Aviation's Role

Due to the proximity of the Manchurian railways,

↻ Major V.M. Zabaluev, Commander of the 70th IAP (to the right) expressing his gratitude to Captain S. Gritsevets for his delivery from enemy troops after he made a forced landing.

◑ Inspection of a Japanese aircraft debris. The plane type is hard to tell from this picture.

including the Chinese Eastern Railway and the Halun Arshan railway terminal, the Japanese were very sparing in using any transport aircraft, either military or civil, and they were employed only for the urgent delivery of special purpose cargos and taking the command staff to the frontier. The Soviet-Mongolian troops were harder to supply with their nearest operable railway terminal 650km away to the North. Therefore the 1st Army Group and their Mongolian allies entirely depended upon automobile and air shipments from the Trans-Baikal Region. In view of shortage of regular trucks, G.K. Zhukov authorised cargo transportation by military truck and even

artillery tractors. Meanwhile, all high-priority shipments were to be delivered by air. However the Mongolians didn't have any transport aircraft, all they had were two single-engine Stahl-3 passenger aircraft, an AIR-6 and one obsolete Junkers. All four aircraft belonged to the Ulan Bator Flying School and were of little use as transport planes. In May 1939, the 19th Transport Squadron (known also as 'Major Egorov's group' or 'Major Egorov's flight') began to form. After the beginning of hostilities, the 113th and 114th squadrons of the 4th TBAP (Heavy Bomber Air Regiment) were withdrawn from Trans-Baikal Military District and eventually relocated to an airfield in the

◐ Ki-27-Otsu of the 64th Regiment's 1st Squadron; the eagle under the canopy is the regiment's emblem.

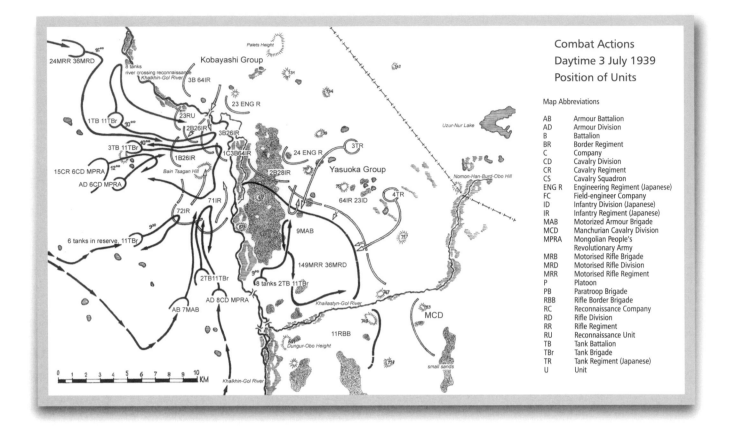

The Japanese 1st Fighter Regiment's pilots, including Lieutenant Masatoshi Masudzava with a reported record of twelve kills in the air at Khalkhin-Gol.

vicinity of Obo Somon in Mongolia. By May 1, seven four-engine TB-3 heavy bombers arrived at the 57th Infantry Corps' Air Force and another four TB-3s were being prepared to leave for Mongolia. These obsolete heavy bombers would be used as cargo planes and came equipped with M-17 power plants that required huge, complicated repairs to keep them flying. Later in May, the squadron strength was finally built up to include 29 ex-heavy bombers. The remaining two squadrons of the 4th TBAP remained in Ukkurey for retraining on the DB-3 long-range bomber. In addition, the 19th Squadron's stock included two TB-1 bombers for local lifting purposes and four R-5 light bombers for liaison. TB-3 carriers performed shuttle flights between Tamtsag Bulak and Chita delivering manpower, weaponry, ammunition, medicines, spare parts and technical supplies to the front line. On 17 August three aircraft arrived with printing equipment that would allow the production of propaganda leaflets in Japanese, Chinese and Mongolian.

During the conflict, the TB-3 transport aircraft delivered a total of 1,885 tons of cargo, of which 60% was weaponry, and carried 7,288 passengers, including the entire technical staff of four fighter regiments (8, 22, 32 and 56th IAP) and one bomber regiment (38th SBAP), pilot personnel of four fighter squadrons (250 pilots), and 400 airborne troops. Passengers included 4,571 injured troops and aviators evacuated on return flights, and a TB-3 without special facilities for the wounded could usually carry six to eight patients with heavy wounds and up to fourteen patients with minor wounds, and a TB-3 re-equipped to serve a flying ambulance could carry twelve patients with heavy wounds and up to six with minor wounds. Stretchers for the wounded would be usually placed in three tiers inside the centre wing alongside the fuel tanks, and other patients could occupy the hull and the wings. Later in July 1939, the Red Army Sanitary Institute prepared a project for a TB-3 redesign as a specialised flying ambulance and asked for a bomber to test the improvements. On 5 August Air Force Headquarters suggested that five such bombers could be withdrawn from the Rzhev Air Division and reworked into air ambulances at Khimky Factory No. 84. The factory, however, lacked the necessary time and resources, and sadly not a single TB-3 underwent such rework. As for the 4th TBAP aircraft, they were custom reworked on-site in a rather primitive manner. During the conflict, the TB-3 carried out over 500 successful transport flights; the only potentially hazardous accident happened on board a TB-3 heading for Chita when the inner engine caught fire, but this was promptly extinguished, and the plane made its way to its destination with the three intact engines. Another noteworthy technical failure episode was a powerplant water-cooler leak in flight. Here the on-board technician had to tie himself to a guard rail and

◑ Ki-27 fighter prepares for take-off.

◑ Ki-21 of the 60th Regiment's 2nd Squadron in preparation for sortie.

Dominoes were among the favorite games played by the Soviet fighter pilots.

Marshal Choibolsan with Mongolian soldiers.

make his way to the leaking engine crawling across the wing surface with a canister of water in one hand and a manual pump in another to refill the cooling system and not let the engine catch fire! The older TB-1 bombers were also used for cargo and personnel transportation and one reported incident shows that when a Soviet I-15bis force landed with engine failure a TB-1 delivered them a spare and a repair crew to help the fighter get back home safely.

Later, the Soviet transport air force in Mongolia was enhanced with a group of modern DC-3 passenger aircraft exported from the USA. They were detached from NII VVS stock, the Air Force special-purpose squadron (at the Soviet generalship's disposal) and the Civil Air Fleet's special-purpose squadron. The group included five or six DC-3s sent from Moscow to Chita where they would be based, but apart from the 19th squadron. These transport aircraft were used for shipping spare parts, ammunition and medicines to Khalkhin Gol. The DC-3 delivered a total 350 tons of cargo and passengers during the conflict and also evacuated the wounded, and these flying ambulances incorporated three-tier stands for medical stretchers carrying eighteen cases per flight. The official appraisal of the rework was very positive: "The 'Douglas' ambulance is very comfortable; the engines are hardly heard;

ventilation and heating systems work; medical staff have free access to the wounded to continuously observe them and provide first aid in flight and every stretcher stand is equipped with an oxygen supply outlet."

Pilot V. Grachev's 'Douglas' was equipped with defensive arms – twin ShKAS machine guns stuck out of the entry door, and another machine gun was installed in one of the window-ports along the opposite sidewall. The only reason for these threatening but absolutely useless installations came at the whim of Stalin's personal representative, the Red Army's Chief Political Administration Head, L.Z. Mekhlis who categorically refused to step aboard 'a defenceless plane'. The only Japanese fighter attack of a DC-3 was reported after the enemy's raid against its home airbase. The pilot, M. Nyukhtikov took his DC-3 off the ground and was followed by a Japanese Ki-27. The transport aircraft, however, survived the pursuit and landed at another field with twenty-two bullet holes. Meanwhile, from its home field the DC-3 and its crew were reported as casualties to Moscow. Eventually, the misreported loss was corrected. Another threat to the DC-3 was Soviet anti-aircraft artillery mistaking an unfamiliar transport aircraft for a Japanese intruder. The transport aircraft were much overused. Usually, they would leave for a Trans-Baikal

◡ Red Army soldiers inspect the debris of bagged Ki-21 bomber.

◖ Red Army soldiers climb over a downed Ki-21.

◖ 'Maxim' quadruple machine guns protected Soviet airfields from enemy air raids.

airbase, load-up – and arrive back in Mongolia the next morning. Here is the record of flights performed within a single day – August 30: 'Two TB-3's left Bain Tumen for Chita and Tamtsag Bulak with loads of food. Later in the day three more TB-3's left for Tamsag with loads of ambulance equipment, followed by a 'Douglas' with food and another 'Douglas' with medication. From Nerchinsk, three more TB-3's left for Tamsag with fresh food with three more being prepared for a flight from Domna to Chita to collect sanitation equipment and medication. In August, the Japanese recognised their defeat and the conflict ceased. All DC-3s survived the campaign and pilots A. Golovanov, V. Grachev, M. Nyukhtikov, Lebedev and Kubyshko, and navigator Ivanov were honoured with the 'Orders of Wartime Red Banner', and the 19th squadron commander Egorov, who also participated in night time raids on Japanese positions, was awarded the 'Order of Lenin'.

Bain Tsagan

By July, the 1st Army Group Air Force included 280 aircraft. A week later a number of new I-153 Chayka ('Seagull') and I-16P (or I-16 Type 17) arrived. The former was the well-known I-15bis biplane with

↻ The obsolete R-6 reconnaissance aircraft were used as trainers for the bi-engined SB bomber and, later, as transports. This photo shows a crashed R-6 transport.

↺ Soviet pilots in front of a DC-3 military transport. Note the blotch-type camouflage.

◑ Two DC-3s on their way from Chita to Ulan Bator. No insignia and the non-standard codes may imply an attempt to misrepresent this Douglas aircraft as Mongolian.

retractable undercarriage, high-altitude M-62 powerplant and four ShKAS machine guns; the latter was an I-16 modification with two ShKAS machine guns and two 20mm ShVAK cannon. The modified I-16P was heavier, slower and clumsier when compared to its predecessor, due to its more powerful weaponry; however, this new fighter now could easily bag a heavy bomber or smash an armoured vehicle and even a light tank. The first to arrive were fifteen 'Seagulls' and they were consolidated as a separate squadron with a number nicknamed of 'Gritsevetz Squadron' – after its

commander Captain S. Gritsevets. Soon after that, a few more dozen Chaykas arrived. They were categorized as 'secret', and their pilots were restricted from crossing the front line. However, the new Seagulls proved to have an inherent defect in their firing synchronization unit that could have resulted in damaged propeller blades, and it took 48 sleepless hours for ground technicians to find and apply a remedy to the problem and make their new warbirds combat-ready. Seven I-16P monoplanes were allocated to the 22nd IAP squadron under Captain E. Stepanov's

↻ DC-3 at Ulan-Bator airfield.

⋂ DC-3 at a frontier airfield, collecting the wounded.

command and they replaced the old I-15bis that were relocated to the air defence service of the airfields, and also could be employed in the role of light attack. Sadly Soviet combat performance was complicated by the airfields' remoteness from Trans-Baikal feeder bases and operational railway depots. Whatever supplies were required had to be delivered by truck, so shortages of fuel were not rare.

By now Soviet intelligence was reporting 312 aircraft at Japanese disposal, which was almost a three-fold overestimation of the actual enemy force, and taking into account earlier losses by July 1,

General Giga had only 100 to 110 aircraft under his command. In June the Japanese consistently relocated their reserves from Hailar area towards the frontier and on July 3, long before dawn, they proceeded to cross the Khalkhin Gol with using pontoon boats, and attacked the Mongolian 6th cavalry division's positions. By sunrise, the Japanese already had a foothold at the Bain Tsagan hill and deployed 10,000 soldiers and 160 artillery pieces. From there, it would be logical to deliver a sweeping flank manoeuvre against the Soviet-Mongolian troops, and indeed two regiments of the 23rd infantry division moved out in

⋃ DC-3 taking off from the Bain Tumen airfield with a TB-3 parked in the background.

↻ The wounded being lifted aboard a DC-3.

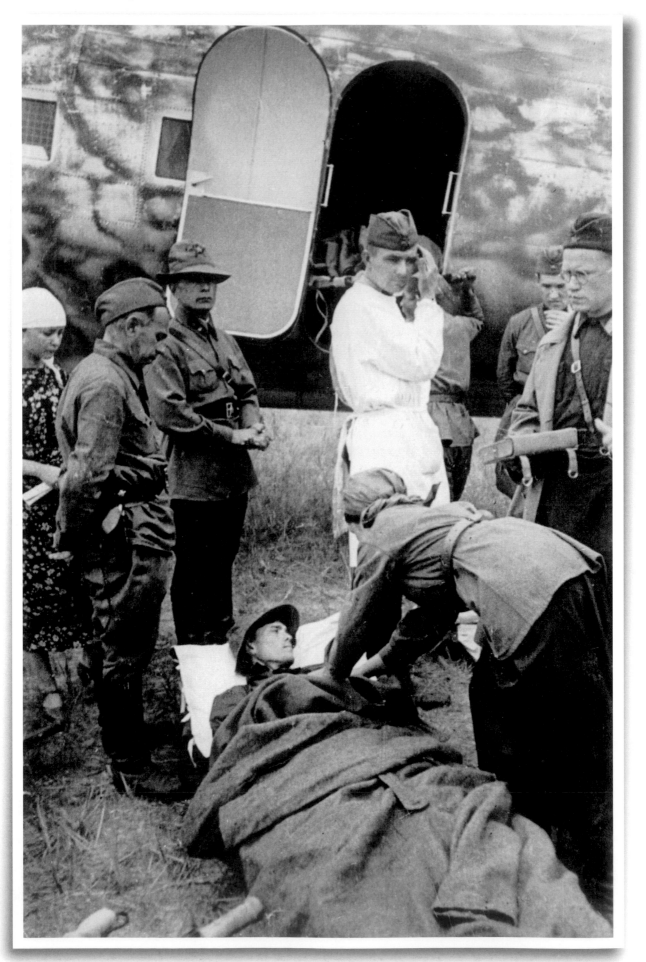

⟳ I-153 biplane fighter.

a southerly direction. G.K. Zhukov promptly sent tanks, armoured vehicles and motorised infantry to meet the intruders. Meanwhile, the heavy artillery opened fire towards the hill, and the air regiments began to take-off on the alert signal. The Mongolian horsemen attempted a counterattack, but were scattered by enemy bomb strikes. The Japanese performed a number of sweeping bombing runs despite the Soviet anti-aircraft fire and fighter attacks, and this resulted in two Ki-15s, a Ki-30 and a Ki-21 being lost. At this point, seventy-three high-speed SB bombers attacked Bain Tsagan. They swept over the hill in a large formation with several squadrons following one another at a distance of 100 to 400m, with some overlap in altitude and a sideways shift, thus forming a 'snake'. The bombers were escorted by I-16 fighters and released FAB-100 and FAB-250 bombs and B.A. Smirnov would later write: 'The SB bombers worked like a smoothly running conveyor belt'.

At the same time a wing of I-15bis fighters of the 22nd IAP began a ground attack on the enemy's infantry and artillery batteries. With machine-gun support, Soviet tanks broke through the Japanese line of defence at which point the SB bombers switched to sweeping the Japanese troops off Nomonhan Burd Obo hill. However, they were met both by anti-aircraft

⋂ DC-3 at Ulan Bator airfield. Note the civil-type (non-Soviet) alphanumeric code on the hull.

 P. Podkolzin, an attack squadron pilot, beside his I-15bis.

 An SB flight and ground crew members (from left to right): Political Instructor K. Shvetsov, the pilot; Senior Lieutenant S. Isaev – navigator; A. Kovalev – motorist; N. Mylnikov – radio gunner and K. Balakin – technician.

⊕ DC-3 navigators I. Dushkin and I. Pryashnikov.

fire and fighters and lost two SB bombers. The Japanese defended the hill desperately for another day, but the outcome had already been predetermined. Massive tank and armoured vehicle attacks forced them back to the east slope – and further towards the river bank where they would have to stop and rail at their own General Kamitsubaru, who had literally burnt the pontoon bridge behind him earlier in the day and thus had cut them off! At this point, the I-16Ps received their first opportunity to test their light cannon in a slaughter-like ground attack. As G.K. Zhukov would vividly recall it in his memoirs, 'thousands of human corpses and horse carcasses, and a mess of smashed cannonry, mortars, machine guns and vehicles were thickly spread on the slope of Bain Tsagan hill'. Many Japanese soldiers sought shelter from Soviet tanks in the river; most of them never reached the home bank. By the end of the battle, the Soviet Command decided to battle-test the I-153

'Gritsevetz' squadron. The Soviet aircraft, however, paid the cost of that victory, as the Japanese troops defended the pontoons furiously and according to Soviet sources, they shot down seven SB bombers (ten crew members killed) and badly damaged two I-16 fighters (both pilots wounded) and one I-16P crashed landed. The Japanese claimed ten bombers, thirty-five fighters and an R-Zet as spoils. Again disparity is found in reports of the Japanese air force losses. Soviet sources buried eleven Ki-27 pilots, while the Japanese would not admit any casualties at all. As for July 5, Soviets reported two SB bombers and five crew lost, while the Japanese claimed five SB and seven I-16 fighters (the latter, apparently, did not take off at all on that day).

Chapter 3
A Period of Relative Inactivity

For the rest of July to the end of August both sides' ground forces stood inactive. The only attack was undertaken by a Japanese regiment on August 12. Supported by aviation, they suddenly pushed the Mongolian 22nd Cavalry regiment a few kilometres back to the south. New infantry, cavalry, artillery and armoured troops were now being drawn towards the Khalkhin Gol theatre and the opposing air forces also built up strength. On the Soviet side, an additional high-speed bomber regiment arrived from Belorussia (56th SBAP of 57 SB aircraft) along with a fighter regiment (56th IAP of 64 I-16, 24 I-153 and 13 I-15bis under Major S.P. Danilov command) and the earlier mentioned TB-3 heavy bomber group. On July 14 1939 a decision was made to send the 49th SBAP to Mongolia. That regiment, however, had to be formed before leaving and manpower was borrowed from three squadrons of the 16th SBAP (Rzhev) and squadrons of the33rd SBAP (Belaya Tserkov). Their crews arrived in Moscow to collect the fifty-three bombers allocated to the new regiment. The aircraft, however, were all second-hand and many were badly worn. However, after some maintenance and repair, on August 23 Colonel Kretov took off from the Central Airfield with his new regiment. However, the 49th SBAP would never participate in the Khalkhin Gol campaign and would stay in Trans-Baikal as a reserve. By July 20, 103 SBs were present in Mongolia, and by August 1 their number had reached 181 aircraft. Later in August, all the SB regiments at Khalkhin Gol were merged into the 100th Air Brigade. The flight personnel were replenished with the best pilots being relocated from all parts of the Soviet Union, including Europe. However, these newcomers were considered as 'just on detachment' from their parent units and thus a combined naval aviation squadron that arrived in Bain Tsagan with I-16 fighters with ten pilots of the Baltic Sea Fleet and five pilots of the Black Sea Fleet were combined under the command of Major Novikov. Direct shipments of brand new I-153 and I-16 fighters were added to the existing stocks, resulting in an overabundance of fighters in the field. For instance, by August the 70th IAP had over 100 aircraft at its pilots' disposal and for that reason the older I-15bis (about sixty aircraft) were transferred to airfield defence groups. The growth of available aircraft also demanded more airfields, and these were promptly constructed. For example, the 70th IAP was redeployed to the new airfield at Ikhe Tashigay Nor within 90km of Tamtsag Bulak.

By 1 August, the Soviet military aviation detachments at Khalkhin Gol included 525 aircraft along with a further seven Mongolian R-5s. The

↻ The 150th Squadron bomber crew (from left to right): Lieutenant A. Churilin, the pilot; A. Anisimov, radio gunner; A. Egorov, navigator.

◖ S. Matrosov, an attack fighter pilot, by his I-15bis.

Japanese also prepared themselves for future combat and by the middle of July, they had concentrated two full air brigades at Khalkhin Gol – the 9th Brigade under Major General I. Simono's command and the 12th Brigade of Major General E. Adzumi. By July 14 these two brigades had 148 aircraft, including thirty-eight bombers, eighty-six fighters and thirty-four single-engined recce aircraft. However, while the Soviet air force's aircraft stock and flight personnel steadily improved in quality, the Japanese continued to use 'old and battered' equipment, such as the Ki-4 air reconnaissance biplanes, which was a clear indication that the Kwantung Army was short of reserves.

By the middle of July, the Japanese detachment in Manchukuo was in fact exhausted and sought reinforcements, which had to be drawn from Central China where the Japanese fought Chiang Kai-shek's army. The 64th fighter regiment (three Ki-27 squadrons) and the 31st light bomber regiment (two Ki-30 squadrons) were withdrawn and relocated to Manchukuo and both wings were manned by

experienced pilots who had fought in China, as for example, the 64th regiment's commander was the famous ace T. Kato. By August, the Japanese had accumulated about 200 aircraft, however yet again Soviet intelligence overestimated their number and reported up to 450 Japanese aircraft, including 252 fighters. During this period of quiet on the ground, hostilities in the air continued. Having smashed the Japanese at Bain Tsagan hill, the SB bombers proceeded to methodically sweep the front line and rear positions. The I-16 and I-15bis fighters also undertook ground attacks on the Japanese front positions and as well as strafing with their machine guns, the I-15bis biplanes would often release small bombs.

On July 6 a wing of twenty-two I-16 and twenty-three I-15bis on their way to a ground-attack mission encountered thirty Ki-27's above Buzur Nor. Again the disparate claims of both sides are quite amazing! The Soviets claimed twenty-one Japanese aircraft shot down for the loss of two I-15bis fighters, and a further eighteen were reported as damaged. The Japanese,

🎧 Ki-4 reconnaissance planes in the field.

however, claimed to have completely destroyed twenty-two I-16 fighters (that is basically all the aircraft of that type that had taken part in the dogfight) and four SB bombers. The only SB lost on July 6 (pilot Krasnykhin) was shot down by Soviet anti-aircraft fire by mistake! The pilot landed his burning bomber on its belly, and the crew escaped

before the aircraft was lost. Such contradictory reports of the numbers of friend and foe aircraft destroyed were typical for the entire period of the conflict as both sides hugely exaggerated the enemy's and understated their own losses. Such contradictions make it difficult to judge the true outcome of the series of heavy dogfights that took place on 9 to 12 July. The largest occurred on July 10 and involved over 100 Soviet and about sixty Japanese fighters. The Soviet reports were rather modest and mentioned eleven shot-down 'Japs' and three I-16 and their pilots lost and another four pilots wounded. Captain Balashov brought his fighter back home despite a severe head wound only to die three days later. The Japanese claimed to have destroyed sixty-four Soviet aircraft and lost a single Ki-27. In reality, by the middle of July Japanese losses began to exceed those of the Soviet side, as for instance Soviet fighters shot down the renowned Japanese ace M. Hamada (with seventeen kills) and forced the 1st regiment's commander Lieutenant Colonel Hamada to bail out of his burning aircraft and land in Mongolian territory. He was rescued by Sergeant T. Matsumura who landed nearby to pick up his commander. By then, the Soviet and the Japanese pilots had pretty well learned each other's skills and weaknesses – for example the Japanese would usually try to engage the Soviet fighters in a horizontal manoeuvre and would skillfully used the clouds or blinding sun to stay undetected until the last moment. The Soviet pilots also made the best use of their I-16's strengths and accelerated their fighters, nose-diving either to get rid of a chasing enemy or gain

↶ A captured Japanese pilot.

↻ The bagged Japanese Ki-27 fighter under scrutiny.

↻ The bagged Japanese Ki-27 fighter under scrutiny.

additional speed before attacking. The Ki-27 was much slower in the dive and this sort of manoeuvre was an unsafe way to accelerate for them as the overload when pulling back to the horizontal could result in collapsed wings.

As a result of the permanent threat of Japanese fighter attacks and anti-aircraft artillery, the SB bombers were ordered to increase bombing altitudes from 2,500 – 3,000m to 6,500 – 7,500m. At that height, the enemy guns were ineffective, and any fighters could reach them in time. On the other hand, the bombing accuracy decreased. Japanese air reconnaissance now made repeated attempts to pinpoint the Soviet air forces' distribution and for that purpose they employed the single-engined Ki-15 after it had demonstrated a good range and speed ,and the older I-15bis airfield defence fighters just could not intercept them. On July 7, four of the newer I-153 biplanes took off trom Tamtsag Bulak field to intercept a Ki-15 hovering high above and supposedly taking snapshots, however by the time they reached combat height, the enemy had gone. The story was repeated daily, but the Chayka biplanes would take off – but fail to intercept the Japanese raider. The idea of airborne alert was considered and rejected for the reason of

inappropriately high engine wear, but later ground observation systems improved, allowing interceptors to take off well in advance. In this case, a reconnaissance aircraft armed with a single machine gun had little chance to survive an attack. In the period from 15 to 21 July, the sky seemed to be clear of any aircraft due to the ongoing redeployments and reinforcements on either side. And on July 22 the largest (in numbers) air dogfight of the entire armed conflict began in the vicinity of Bain Hoshu hill. The estimates of the combatant aircraft number from 200 to 300. The number of Soviet fighters is clearly revealed: 157 (ninety-five I-16 and sixty-two I-15bis) fighters and as for the Japanese involvement, western sources estimate their air power as 'more than forty fighters', while the Soviet ones offer an estimate of 130 – 150. It is clear now that the former figure is closer to the truth than the latter, which might have been invented for the purposes of propaganda. The 'grand dogfight' at Bain Hoshu continued for an hour and a half before events turned into a series of smaller dogfights and finally dissipated. Soviet pilots reported twelve enemy fighters shot down, their Japanese counterparts – thirty-nine. However, the actual documented losses investigated and reported by a

The Soviet Air Force Detachment Commander Y.V. Smushkevich demonstrates a torn-off piece of canvas from a downed Japanese aircraft's tailfin to the 1st Army Group's General Staff. Second in on right is the Army Group's Commander G.K. Zhukov.

⊂ The Japanese pilots of the 11th Regiment's 1st Squadron demonstrate their spoils of war – a Soviet parachute and a TT handgun. Major K. Simada, the Squadron Commander (in the foreground), and Sergeant B. Yesiyama (in the background, with the gun in his hands) would be killed on 15 September in a mass dogfight.

Soviet historian V. Kondratyev amounted to five I-15bis lost by the Red Army Air Force and four Ki-27 lost by the Japanese. The first case of ram attack was reported here when Senior Lieutenant V. Skobarikhin hit an enemy fighter with his left wing in order to protect his wingman, Senior Lieutenant V. Vuss. Some authors add that Skobarikhin even tried to continue the fight after the ram attack, but his fighter was too badly damaged, so he withdrew and safely returned home. Four Soviet pilots died and three were wounded and all four Japanese flyers shot down escaped by parachutes. Three of them found their way home, but the fourth shot himself to avoid being captured.

On July 23 the 56th IAP entered the combat for the first time, although their debut was not successful. While dominating the enemy in numbers in the proportion 3:2, the Soviet pilots shot down one Japanese fighter and lost two of their own. Meanwhile, the both sides' bombers continued their raids on ground targets. On July 23 Ki-21 and Ki-30 bombers performed 128 sorties and dropped forty-eight tons of bombs, and taking into account that the Japanese had no more than forty bombers at their disposal, each crew had two perform at least three sorties. On July 24 a group of Ki-30s was attacked by fighters from the 22nd IAP and lost two bombers. The Soviet SB bombers were much more numerous and could fly sparingly; for instance, on July 31 according to reports they delivered 27.5 tons of bombs and if you divide that figure by the nominal bomb-load of an SB, you can see that the Soviet bombers performed about fifty sorties on that day. On July 23 thirty-two Ki-27 fighters attempted an attack on an SB group, but were repelled by twenty-seven I-16s and one I-153. The

bombers continued and the fighters clashed, the outcome being five Japanese and one Soviet fighter shot down. The permanent threat of enemy fighter attack resulted in up to fifty fighters escorting every bomber group. By July 27 the 150th SBAP had lost a total of four SB bombers as a result of enemy fighter attacks, and three were destroyed by fire in air. The

⊃ The 22nd IAP Commissar V.N. Kalachev by his I-153.

⋂ Senior Lieutenant V. Skobarikhin in his cockpit after a ram attack; clearly visible is the damage to the left wing.

38th SBAP's losses were not so painful: one bomber shot down and two bombers missing. The above statistics seem to ignore the two SBs colliding above a target on July 24.

Within the air regiments, aircraft of different series were packed together, including those with the M-100A and the M-103 power plants. As a result during any 'joint flight', the older bombers' performance limited the freedom of others to speed up or perform evasive manoeuvres, leaving the entire group more vulnerable both to the enemy fighters and the anti-aircraft fire. The SB's weaponry also proved to be inefficient as the two front machine guns appeared excessive and were scarcely used, while the aircraft's rear lacked enough fire power to protect it from the fighters' attacks. Many gunners would have preferred twin-guns to the existing single ShKAS mounted in the Tur-9 turret. The machine gun at the belly port was not used at all, the reason being that the radio operator/gunner of an SB had to serve either the upper or the bottom mount. Switching position would leave the aircraft defenceless for too long, and the gunners tended to stick to the upper machine gun

⋂ Ki-27 in the field: the 'lightning-shaped' insignia on the vertical tail implies that this aircraft belonged to the 11th Air Regiment.

as the more effective one. Reworked aircraft were the exception as they were equipped with a triggering mechanism that allowed for firing with the bottom machine gun from the top gun position and a special handle pulled the bottom gun's trigger through a Bowden cable release mechanism. The bombers were also poorly equipped with communication equipment – both internal and aircraft-to-aircraft and aircraft-to-ground. In order to avoid radio interception and false commands by the enemy, the Soviet commanders ordered the removal of all of radio equipment, and the intercoms were sealed off after a case reported that a radio-gunner, having smelled some smoke, misinterpreted the pilot's 'all OK' message and bailed out, while the aircraft safely proceeded back to its airbase. The pneumatic tube message transfer system that was supposed to support communication between the navigator and the radio-gunner was unreliable to the extent of being complete useless. The Soviet fighters did not have any radios at all. The leader usually gave orders to the wingmen with the use of gestures and/or rocking wings. The 'follow me' principle dominated, i.e., the wingmen just replicated every manoeuvre of the leader. From the ground, commands were usually laid out with Popham panels or shot up in a series of colored flares. Flare guns were also used for sending feedback messages from the aircraft, and inefficient communications would remain the 'Achilles' heel' of Soviet military aviation for years.

The Japanese tried out kytoons (balloons) for the purposes of artillery gunfire adjustment. The solution proved to be a complete failure in an environment rich with Soviet fighters. Zhukov ordered the pilots to 'cut those sausages', and the last report about a hot-air balloon shot down by the 70th IAP commander's flight Major G. Kravchenko was dated July 25. Mass dogfights continued and one of them resulted in the Japanese 11th Regiment's 1st Squadron commander S. Kadzima being forced to land in a Soviet-controlled area due to a fuel line disruption. The officer was rescued by another pilot, and his almost intact aircraft was captured by the Red Army and shipped to the Soviet Union. On 10 September the Ki-27 was delivered to NII VVS test airfield and after minor repairs and a powerplant replacement, the Ki-27 was subjected to a series of ground and flight tests. On July 29 Soviet aviation used the tactics that had previously been successfully tested in Spain where 22nd IAP fighters delivered a series of ground strikes on the enemy airfields. At dawn, twenty I-16 (armed with both machine guns and cannon) swept the advanced Alai airfield 8km to the north of Lake Uzur Nor. This low-altitude attack caught by surprise eleven Ki-27 aircraft taxiing towards the runway, and two Japanese fighters exploded and the other nine suffered damage. Some two hours later the raid was repeated when the Japanese aircraft were on approach to their

○ Ki-27 engine servicing.

○ Pilot V. Skobarikhin in front of his I-16 Type 10 fighter.

☊ Red Army soldiers inspect a downed Ki-27 of the 1st Regiment's 1st Squadron. Soviet sources claimed that it was the one brought down by the ram attack of pilot V. Skobarikhin.

landing field. This second attack resulted in three Ki-27 being shot down in the air. After that the I-16's strafed the service areas inflicting the maximum possible damage to aircraft, airfield facilities and ground personnel. As the result, the Japanese 24th Regiment reported six fighters as lost and another five as badly damaged.

Probably as an act of revenge for the damage, a few hours later a large group of Japanese fighters crossed the river and engaged with Soviet pilots. The outcome of this mass dogfight was hardly satisfactory for the Japanese, and while they claimed to have shot down fifty Soviet aircraft, in fact the Air Force 1st Army Group lost two I-16 and one I-15bis fighters and one pilot. And the Japanese confirmed losses were four Ki-27 and all the four pilots, including the 1st Regiment commander Major F. Harada (17 wins). An unconfirmed version is that Harada parachuted down, was captured and killed during his attempt to escape. Soviet literature sources also mention a mythical Colonel Takeo as shot down by pilot V. Rakhimov and captured after parachuting down. However, neither Soviet nor Japanese military reports contain any evidence in support of that episode's authenticity. The most remarkable event of August 3 was the 56th IAP

☋ The Soviet aces Captain S. Gritsevets (in the I-153 cockpit) and G. Kravchenko.

squadron commander Major V.P. Kustov's ram attack on 'an enemy two-engined bomber' (a Ki-21 perhaps). Both aircraft crashed killing their crews and Major Kustov was honored with the title of 'Hero of the Soviet Union'. On August 5, another act of heroism was accomplished by the 150th SBAP Commissar M.A. Yuyukin. During a bombing raid on Japanese storehouses, two Soviet squadrons were attacked by enemy fighters who sheltered behind a murderous anti-aircraft firewall. When a shell burst resulted in his left engine exploding Yuyukin ordered his crew to escape and then he flew his burning bomber, with a full load of bombs, into the Japanese anti-aircraft battery (or an ammunition depot, according to some other sources). The interesting fact is that among the aircrew of Yuyukin's SB during that mission was Nicolay F. Gastello who occupied the navigator's seat. Being the commander of a TB-3 flight, Gastello replaced Yuyukin's regular navigator in order to perform a daytime reconnaissance of the target area before the planned night raid of his own. After parachuting down in the Japanese rear, he and his radio-gunner

↷ Japanese inspect an SB bomber's wing.

Razboynikov engaged in a firefight fight with the Japanese, which Gastello survived, unlike his less fortunate comrade. Years later, in the course of the World War II, Gastello would replicate Yuyukin's manoeuvre and crash his knocked-down DB-3F with its full load of bombs into a German armoured convoy.

↷ A captured Japanese S. Kadzima's Ki-27 being prepared to be towed away.

On the same day, a number of dogfights took place where the Russians claimed seventeen shot down for the loss of a single I-16, whereas the Japanese reported the score of thirty-seven to two in their favour. What is clear was that the famous Japanese ace M. Motodzima was killed.

The Mongolian Debut

Despite the fact the warfare took place in Mongolia, initially the MPR Air Force took little or no part in it. While Mongolian infantrymen, horsemen and even armoured vehicles were involved in combat operations right from the beginning of the conflict, native pilots didn't join until as late as the middle of July. The reasons behind this included poor flight training and the Mongolian Air Force's outdated aircraft. Their obsolete R-5 biplanes would be easy targets in a sky swarming with enemy fighters and could be used only in night-time. However, the Mongol pilots lacked night skills and it therefore took some time to organize and conduct a retraining program for the local crews.

After that a local flight group was formed with pilot Bor as the commander, and initially included eight aircraft. Due to the lack of skilled Mongolian aviators, teams now included Soviet instructors and advisors, and the aircraft's identification markings too were all Soviet. The first mission of the Mongolians took place on July 13 when three R-5 light bombers took off from Matad airfield. The leading R-5, however, was piloted by the Soviet officer Zaysanov, with a long record of service as an advisor to the MPR Air Force. The 'night owls' usual tactics were as follows: at dusk, they made the leg from Matad to Hamar Dabaa advanced field to refuel and rearm. From there, the bombers would depart towards their objectives around midnight. For pilot orientation, a series of the 'bats' (kerosene lamps with a focused beam) were placed along Khalkhin Gol, 3 to 7 km away from the front line, with the beam directed away from the enemy. These 'bats' were placed within 500m of one another resulting in a 50 metre-long arrow indicating the direction of the river valley towards the enemy's rear. The flight's task was

I-16 coming in to land.

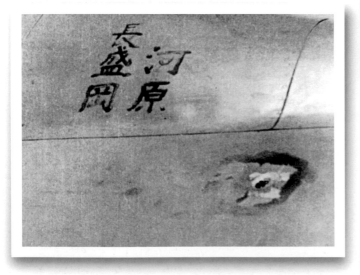

A puncture hole in S. Kadzima's fighter's fuselage with Japanese inscription: 'The riverhead lies deep in the mountain ravine'.

The Mongolian air regiment's commander
C. Shagdasuren among Soviet military advisors, including
V. Sudets (to the left).

The captured Ki-27 at the NII VVS test field.

U In late 1930s, the TB-3 four-engine heavy bomber was used as a multi-purpose aircraft designed to deliver day and night bomb strikes and also served as a military transport.

to awaken the Japanese troops night after night and demoralise their soldiers by lack of sleep. Along with this demoralising effect, the air-engines and bomb explosions masked the noise produced by the Soviet troops along the front line. Every R-5 carried a number of light blast bombs and released them one by one as the bombers approached the target area, with a time interval of 10 to 15 minutes in-between. Having released a portion of its load, a bomber would swerve aside for the next, and thus the Bor's squadron made it 'hell' for two nights in a row for the Japanese troops in the vicinity of Jinjing Sume and Depden Sume. When the campaign ended in September, the 'night owls' had undertaken some 165 sorties and released about sixty tons of bombs. The only casualty among them was an R-5 lost to the weather.

TB-3 Night Raids

While the Soviet troops continued preparing for the major offensive, six TB-3 heavy bombers of the 'Yegorov Group' from Obo Somon airfield joined the night raids. Their first mission was accomplished on the night of 19 to 20 August when they approached their target in waves, wing by wing, using the same on-ground flare signals for the direction as the Mongolian R-5 light bombers. Later one-by-one flying tactics would be used and some six to twenty sorties per night were performed by the TB-3 bombers, each carrying a 1,300kg load of assorted explosives. The target was usually illuminated with an SAB flare suspended by the leader; after that, the wing would perform a bombing pass from 1,000 to 1,500m high, which the Japanese anti-aircraft fire could not reach.

O A Mongolian crew of the R-5. Note the single DA machine gun installed in the rear compartment instead of the regular twin-gun mount.

The only reported case of any damage incurred was by pilot L. Varochkin's TB-3 which successful landed at its home airfield with its inner right engine damaged and holes in the fuselage caused by an anti-aircraft shell explosion. The only TB-3 of the night bombers' group lost before the Japanese surrender on September 15 was a TB-3 that crashed on landing due to a mechanical fault. The Air Force 1st Army Group's report read that 'the practice of heavy night-bombing at the second stage proved to be very successful in the absence of any night fighters and searchlights on the enemy side. Such raids produced a substantial moral and tangible damage to the enemy'.

Chapter 4
The Soviet Offensive

While the Japanese concentrated their efforts on reinforcing their defences on the eastern bank of Khalkhin Gol, the Soviet 1st Army Group's command, encouraged by Moscow, was eager to sweep the enemy back beyond the pre-conflict border. Two rifle divisions, a tank brigade, two field artillery regiments and other detachments were brought into the theatre from the USSR. The Air Force was also reinforced.

The bombardment component, i.e. the 100th Air Brigade, included three regiments – the 150th, the 38th and the 56th and earlier in the summer, all three were based at Arjagalanta Hid airfield, 45 km south-east of Matad Somon. In preparation to the offensive, the 38th SBAP was relocated to 'Saratov' airfield, 25km away from Tamtsag Bulak while the 56th and 150th regiments staged to 'Ivanovo' airfield which was prepared for them – also in the neighbourhood of Tamtsag Bulak. The fighter component in Mongolia was reinforced with the 8th and the 32nd IAP. However, both the regiments were ordered to stay in reserve and were to be transferred to the 1st Army Group's Air Force only if the planned offensive operations stalled. The fighter regiments' stocks were

Soviet tanks and troops accumulate in a hollow before attacking the enemy.

replenished with the newest I-16 Type 18 fighters powered M-62 engines and equipped with quadruple ShKAS machine guns with armour-protected fuel tanks and pilot seats. While demonstrating a similar horizontal speed, the new Soviet fighter excelled the Japanese Ki-27 in many other aspects, including its firepower and combat survivability. Moreover, many

Japanese Ki-34, which was often mistaken for a friendly DC-3 by Soviet aviators.

◑ The remains of a Ki-27 fighter in August 1939.

of the older I-16 type 10 aircraft were immediately re-engineered using spare M-62 power plants. With the earlier experience of the Japanese air-to-ground attacks, the fighters were dispersed to the field perimeters with 300 metres spacing between them. The aircraft stood flight-ready with full fuel tanks and ammunition on board. Yet another surprise for the Japanese was being prepared as Soviet fighters would deliver the ever first strike with RS-82 rocket-propelled projectiles. Air Factory No. 21 in Gorky (now Nizhny Novgorod) manufactured six I-16 aircraft with four rocket-launcher rails under each wing using metal foil instead of a fabric covering for the lower wing panels.

Pilots and engineers were selected to operate this new weaponry after special training at a range near Moscow, and before leaving for Mongolia they met the People's Commissar of Defence, K.E. Voroshilov. On August 16, a flight of five I-16s carrying RS-82s under the command of Captain N.I. Zvonarev joined the 22nd IAP. In general, by August 19 the numbers of Soviet and Mongolian aircraft in the conflict area had reached their peak. In order to prepare the 1st Army Group's Air Force for the intensive operations during the offensive, enormous quantities of fuel and lubricants, spare parts and ammunition had to be delivered from the USSR. The ammunition arsenal

◑ A 38th Medium Bomber Regiment's SB after a forced landing. Note the 'typical for the Khalkhin-Gol conflict period' spotted camouflage painted over the regular light-grey or silvery colours.

⋂ I-16 after a forced landing. The wide paint strip near the tail was intended for easier recognition.

alone was estimated at 6,500 metric tonnes and by mid-August the fleet of trucks allocated for these purposes was increased by half. For example, 375 additional fuel-tank trucks joined the 912 already shuttling the Mongolian routes. At the beginning of the offensive, up to ten ammunition refills and fifteen fuel refills per aircraft had been allocated at the front line storage areas.

On August 19, the 22nd IAP fighters delivered a ground attack on the Japanese 64th air regiment's field and destroyed two Ki-27 aircraft without suffering any damage. Later in the day, the SB flight bombed the Halun Arshan rail terminal and thus squeezed the main channel of cargo delivery to the Japanese and Manchukuo troops at Khalkhin Gol. Along with supplies, the enemy forces were also being deprived of fresh manpower. On August 20, at dawn, Soviet artillery began suppressing the Japanese anti-aircraft batteries along the front line and lobbing smoke shells to indicate the targets for the bombers. The SB crew teams stood by their command posts waiting for the order to commence and as soon as they were received, they were promptly delivered to their aircraft by car and started their engines. With a red signal flare fired into the air the bombers would start a straight-forward run directly from their positions and take off without taxiing. The first strike was delivered by 150 to 153 bombers (the available sources slightly disagree about the exact number) escorted by 144 fighters. The bombers were divided into nine-aircraft flights. The first eight flights headed to the Khailastyn Gol's bank to bomb enemy artillery batteries and troops and were intended to trigger the anti-aircraft batteries. So, these

⋂ Lieutenant Hiroshi Sekiguchi of the 64th Regiment; the Japanese claimed that he shot down four Soviet planes at Khalkhin-Gol.

bombers approached from different directions at tree-top height. The Japanese then opened fire revealing the exact location of their batteries, which were immediately attacked by twenty-five I-16P lighter fighter strikers supported by long-range artillery fire from friendly positions.

And after that, one echelon of the main SB group approached the target area at between 4,000 to 5,000m without anti-aircraft fire distracting them. The entire

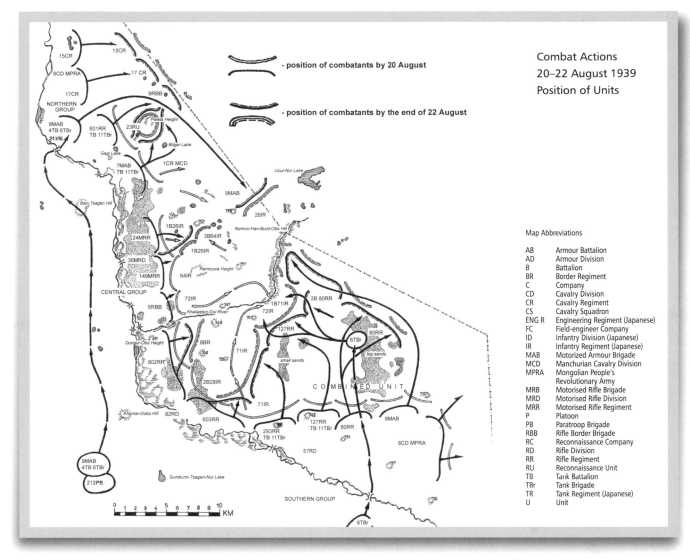

Combat Actions
20–22 August 1939
Position of Units

- position of combatants by 20 August

- position of combatants by the end of 22 August

Map Abbreviations

AB	Armour Battalion
AD	Armour Division
B	Battalion
BR	Border Regiment
C	Company
CD	Cavalry Division
CR	Cavalry Regiment
CS	Cavalry Squadron
ENG R	Engineering Regiment (Japanese)
FC	Field-engineer Company
ID	Infantry Division (Japanese)
IR	Infantry Regiment (Japanese)
MAB	Motorized Armour Brigade
MCD	Manchurian Cavalry Division
MPRA	Mongolian People's Revolutionary Army
MRB	Motorised Rifle Brigade
MRD	Motorised Rifle Division
MRR	Motorised Rifle Regiment
P	Platoon
PB	Paratroop Brigade
RBB	Rifle Border Brigade
RC	Reconnaissance Company
RD	Rifle Division
RR	Rifle Regiment
RU	Reconnaissance Unit
TB	Tank Battalion
TBr	Tank Brigade
TR	Tank Regiment (Japanese)
U	Unit

↻ Soviet and Mongolian soldiers take photos amidst the debris of a crashed Japanese Ki-21 bomber.

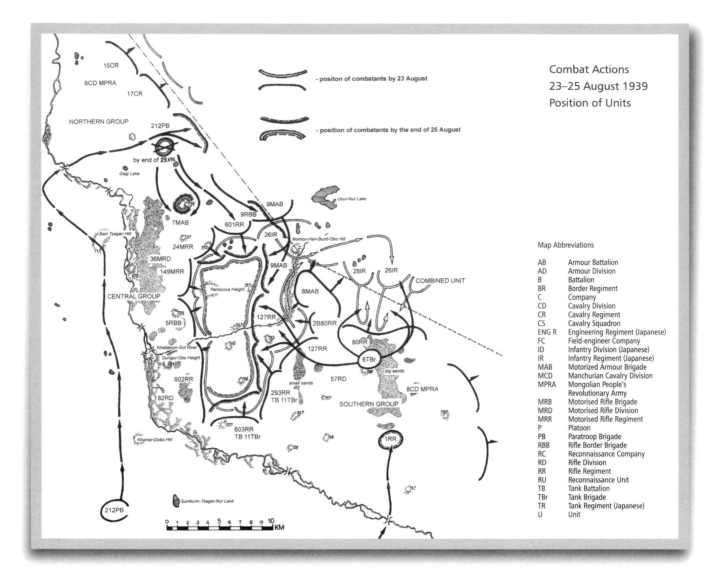

Combat Actions
23–25 August 1939
Position of Units

- positon of combatants by 23 August

- position of combatants by the end of 25 August

Map Abbreviations

AB	Armour Battalion
AD	Armour Division
B	Battalion
BR	Border Regiment
C	Company
CD	Cavalry Division
CR	Cavalry Regiment
CS	Cavalry Squadron
ENG R	Engineering Regiment (Japanese)
FC	Field-engineer Company
ID	Infantry Division (Japanese)
IR	Infantry Regiment (Japanese)
MAB	Motorized Armour Brigade
MCD	Manchurian Cavalry Division
MPRA	Mongolian People's Revolutionary Army
MRB	Motorised Rifle Brigade
MRD	Motorised Rifle Division
MRR	Motorised Rifle Regiment
P	Platoon
PB	Paratroop Brigade
RBB	Rifle Border Brigade
RC	Reconnaissance Company
RD	Rifle Division
RR	Rifle Regiment
RU	Reconnaissance Unit
TB	Tank Battalion
TBr	Tank Brigade
TR	Tank Regiment (Japanese)
U	Unit

raid took the Japanese by complete surprise, and they failed to bring up a single fighter to meet the formation. The bomber squadrons approached in a zig-zag train and 'dive-accelerated' before bombing their targets. At the same time another echelon from the main group performed horizontal bombing passes at 7,000 – 7,500m. The 1st Army's Air Force command reported 'the SB bombers had a good on-target performance from different heights'. Along with the Japanese front line positions, the nearest airfields were also swept. A few hours later, another mass bombing raid was performed and again, the bomb passes began some fifteen minutes after an artillery bombardment. The second mission was performed by 52 SB bombers and 162 to 167 (depending on the sources) fighters. The second echelon's targets were the Japanese fortifications in Khailastyn Gol valley. After these massive air strikes, the entire east bank of Khalkhin Gol was hardly visible as smoke and dust filled the air. The second air offensive, however, met some resistance from Japanese fighters that had managed to slip through the escort and damaged three Soviet SB aircraft. One bomber returned home and landed with one engine destroyed and over 500 hull holes! A

second SB required medium-scale repairs after its main-gear leg collapsed on landing. The third bomber returned with multiple holes only and also required some repair jobs. The Japanese, however, reported that thirty-three fighters and two bombers had been shot down. The thick mist over the landing sites could have resulted in heavier losses and the flat terrain could also be a blessing – or a curse – as in the case of a pilot who almost overturned at the end of the runway as the result of his undercarriage wheel catching in a marmot hole. Having left the plane stuck in the nose-down/tail-up position, the pilot found himself surrounded by a group of Mongol motor troopers – also astray in the thick mist. The Mongols helped the pilot to bring the fighter back into the horizontal position and offered him a sledge-hammer to reshape the fighter's propeller. And, after some little effort, he took off for home!

Mounting Pressure

Later in the day, the Soviet fighters revisited the Japanese 64th Air Regiment's advanced field and destroyed five more Ki-27 fighters and a two-engined transport aircraft (reported as a Douglas by the Soviets, while, in fact, it must have been a Japanese Ki-34) whilst another nine Japanese fighters suffered substantial damage. After the second raid, the Japanese withdrew their surviving aircraft to Gandjur airbase, which resulted in a lessening of the Japanese air force's capability to swiftly respond to any ground forces' requests. What is important, however, Japanese sources do not confirm that this was the loss of the four Ki-27 fighters that the Soviets reported as shot down, including the two destroyed with by use of RS-82 rocket projectiles. Some sources, however, imply that the first combat application of these rockets actually took place three days earlier. Soviet aviation now proceeded to support the ground troops' assault from the air, as the First Army Group intended to encircle the Japanese with synchronised flank strikes. On August 21, at dawn, bombers made nine passes over ground targets at Jinjing Sume, Depden Sume, Burd Obo and lakes Uzur Nor and Janhu. A little later, thirty-six SBs bombed the Khalun Arshan railway depot, and another eighteen swept a large infantry grouping at Tandjur. That day also saw the largest loss of Soviet bombers in the campaign. Five cases were reported: two bombers were shot down by Japanese fighters; two by anti-aircraft batteries and one was reported as missing (later found crashed). Apparently the bombers had performed their missions without the support of the special 'fighter task forces' who were trained to suppress the anti-aircraft batteries. Another factor was that they were flying at 1,200 – 2,000m which also made them vulnerable to small-arms fire. A fifth and final SB was lost to ground fire after the

⋒ The Soviet Air Force Commander at Khalkhin-Gol Y.V. Smushkevich is happy with his subordinates and their performance.

⋓ Engineer I. Prachik (second to the left) and the pilots Captain S. Gritsevets, Major G. Kravchenko, Korobov and Smirnov (left to right).

♩ Soviet pilots by an I-16 fighter at an advanced airfield.

Japanese aviation's counterattack on the airfield in the vicinity of Tamtsag Bulak.

This time Tokyo seemed to have authorised counterstrikes against the Soviet airfields. The situation dictated the need to forget their earlier precautions and these raids were carried out by twenty-four Ki-30, twelve Ki-21 and fifteen Ki-36 bombers under cover of eighty-eight Ki-27 fighters from four regiments. The first wave reached the front line at dawn and early observation post reports allowed for the swift interception of the Japanese aircraft by the Soviet fighters, and a mass dogfight 15 to 25 km to the north of Tamtsag Bulak broke out. Soviet sources report the engagement of 123 I-16, fifty-one I-153 and thirty I-15bis fighters; eleven enemy fighters and two bombers brought down; three I-153 and three I-16 fighters lost; with three Soviet pilots killed and another three bailing out. The vast majority of the Japanese fighters were repelled from Tamtsag Bulak, however a few managed to get through and release their bombs. An hour later, a second wave of Japanese aircraft approached. This raid was much smaller – only around twenty-five aircraft. Thirty-two I-16s of the 56th IAP took of to meet them and, and having driven back the escorting fighters, shot down three bombers. In the

♩ A captured Japanese 20mm type 98 automatic gun that could be used as an anti-aircraft or anti-armour weapon.

afternoon, an 'accidental engagement' was reported when fifty-eight I-16s and eleven I-153s, on their way to a ground-attack mission, encountered a flight of fifteen Japanese bombers escorted by twenty-five fighters. The Soviet pilots just could not miss this opportunity and aborted the ground-attack mission for

♠ Ki-27 fighter in flight.

♠ The 11th Regiment's Ki-27 skeleton.

a more promising dog-fight. As a result the bewildered Japanese lost three Ki-30 bombers and seven accompanying fighters. In the evening, the situation repeated itself as fifty-two I-16 and eight I-153 fighters ran into a group about sixty Japanese aircraft. In this case, however, the parity in numbers resulted in a parity of kills: two Japanese aircraft and one I-16 went down. August 21 was the record-breaking day in the conflict from the standpoints of dogfight intensity and the total number of sorties flown' and while the Japanese reported sixty-five Soviet fighters and nineteen bombers shot down, the actual losses of the 1st Army Group's Air Force amounted to just five SB bombers and seven fighters.

On August 22 a group of Ki-30 bombers took off early in the morning to attack Soviet positions and were intercepted whilst still in Japanese territory. Instead of pressing on with their mission they engaged in a dogfight and lost two Ki-30s and five Ki-27s, – reported by the Soviet pilots as shot down. The rest were forced to release their bombs and flee. The second group of a dozen Ki-21 bombers was also met by nine I-16 and eight I-153 fighters, which attacked the bombers regardless of 'a 15 to 20 Ki-27 fighter escort' and forced them to release their bombs aimlessly before fleeing. This time the I-16s pursued the enemy and brought one bomber down. The Japanese later acknowledged the loss of one Ki-21, one Ki-15 and two Ki-27 aircraft. One of the latter fighters took the life of a renowned Japanese ace K. Motomura

◐ Front-line command post officers observe an air combat engagement.

(fourteen kills). Despite the obvious failures of that day, the Japanese command announced that nine Soviet fighters and three bombers had been destroyed; however the Soviet side had not lost a single aircraft on that day. On the next the bulk of Soviet aviation was operating at Lake Uzur Nor and the noose was almost closed. SB bombers performed a total of fifty-four sorties – all under fighter cover, and the Japanese claimed to have shot down three bombers, while the only confirmed loss was Major Semenov's SB of the 150th SBAP brought down by Japanese anti-aircraft artillery. In the following days, Soviet bombers performed primarily reconnaissance missions with occasional bombing – in fact they enjoyed an unlimited freedom to hunt in the allotted areas. On the following day five, nine-bomber flights swept the Japanese positions at Depden Sume; Japanese anti-aircraft artillery, however, shot two bombers down, but it might be that these were the same two SBs destroyed by Soviet fighters by mistake. Soviet sources often mention this episode – Captain Zvonarev reported that his fighters had shot down two Japanese SB-97 (Soviet nomenclature for the Ki-21) bombers with RS-82 rocket projectiles. He must have misinterpreted and/or misreported the episode as in fact, on August 25 the five I-16 fighters equipped with

rocket projectiles under Captain N.I. Zvonarev's command met nine two-engined Japanese bombers 'to the right of Lake Uzur Nor'. Zvonarev signalled the attack and led his fighters towards the supposed enemy, which he reported to be 'similar to the Japanese SB-96' (Soviet reference for the G3M). However, having approached, he saw the Soviet red star insignia and wing-signalled 'cease fire' – unfortunately, too late as some RS-82's were already on their way to the targets. The bombers were on their way back from a mission over the Japanese positions at Jinjing Sume. Lieutenant V. Fedosov confessed to his error in firing on a friendly target, however, he vouched that he had launched the two RS-82 rockets in the direction of the leader bomber only. The flight commander Zvonarev told the same story and witnessed that he had seen only one bomber falling out of the sky. The investigation resulted in Lieutenant Fedosov being suspended, but not arrested. Two days later, Burmistrov's navigator, Galyshev reported that he had parachuted out of the uncontrollably falling aircraft, but that the other five crew members of the two unlucky bombers were still reported as missing. Galyshev said that their flight was attacked both by the Japanese anti-aircraft artillery and fighters, and the latter were immediately repelled by the escorting I-153 counterparts. And he did not mention any projectiles at all! Probably, he mistook the RS-82's payload explosion for anti-aircraft fire. As Major M.F. Burmistrov's aircraft debris was left on the enemy side of the front line, no technical investigation could be conducted. Corps Commander Y.V. Smushkevich finally lifted Fedosov's suspension ordering him back to Zvonarev's wing. The only punishment suffered by the unlucky pilot would come later when he would be awarded a 'For Courage' medal 'only', while the other pilots would receive the 'Orders of Battle Red Banner'.

The total losses suffered by the Japanese on August 25 were much heavier as both sides undertook their highest level of activity. The Japanese made desperate attempts to prevent the Soviet and Mongolian troops from closing the 'noose', and the Soviet fighters did their best to repel them from the area. Six large-scale air combats (with fifty or more fighters involved) were reported. The biggest one occurred at Yanghu where seventy-six I-16 and thirty-two I-153 fighters attacked about eighty Ki-27s. Soviet documents report fifteen Japanese fighters as shot down without loss but Japanese bombers, however, managed to deliver strikes on Soviet front line positions at the cost of six Ki-30s. A total of forty-eight enemy aircraft were reported as shot down on

♩ Senior Political Instructor P. Selyutin in front of an I-15bis biplane, used as a ground-attack aircraft in the campaign.

August 25 – but the figure is obviously exaggerated. However, the Japanese confirmed the death of aces E. Suzuki (eleven kills) and E. Yadzima (sixteen kills) on that day. The Japanese troops undertook repeated attempts to break out of the 'noose' – all were fruitless as the Soviet-Mongolian troops steadily parried them and efficiently suppressed any pockets of resistance. The Soviet bombers' flight intensity remained extremely high throughout this offensive period and

♩ This 70th IAP's I-153 has overturned in a landing accident.

during the eleven days of the offensive, SB bombers performed more sorties than during the preceding two months. By then, the Soviet pilots had received enough practice in detecting and avoiding the enemy's anti-aircraft batteries. In the vicinity of an anti-aircraft battery they would stretch into a wedge formation or scatter. Another trick they had learned was one of approaching the target from out of the sun or from inside clouds. Sometimes an SB flight would literally 'fall down' like huge metal rain droplets from the clouds towards the target. Or sometimes, when the sky was clear, they would crawl towards the target at minimum height and idle speed and once they had released their bombs they would exit at their maximum cruise speed. Because they did not have sufficient fighters the Japanese had to withdraw their obsolete aircraft equipment from their reserves and the 33rd Regiment was brought into action at Khalkhin Gol with its Ki-10 biplanes, which were absolutely helpless in standing against the Soviet I-16 and I-153 fighters. By the end of August, they had no more than 160 operable aircraft at their disposal and in the face this aircraft shortage, the Japanese command was forced to rely upon the somewhat unmerciful exploitation of whatever was left, resulting in many in-flight failures and much pilot fatigue.

Japanese pilot Captain I. Sakai would later recall in his memoirs: "I had to perform four to six sorties daily. By the evening, I would be usually so tired as to hardly see the landing ground. And the enemy fighters

The Japanese 24th Regiment's pilots stand beside an auto-starter. To the left is Corporal K. Kira with a reported nine kills at Khalkhin-Gol.

Ki-27 fighters of the 59th Regiment's 2nd Squadron.

Ki-27-Otsu in flight.

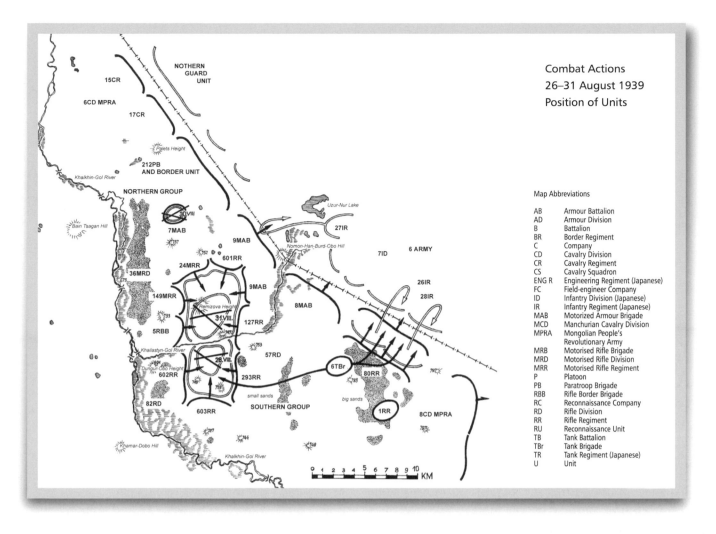

Combat Actions
26–31 August 1939
Position of Units

Map Abbreviations

AB	Armour Battalion
AD	Armour Division
B	Battalion
BR	Border Regiment
C	Company
CD	Cavalry Division
CR	Cavalry Regiment
CS	Cavalry Squadron
ENG R	Engineering Regiment (Japanese)
FC	Field-engineer Company
ID	Infantry Division (Japanese)
IR	Infantry Regiment (Japanese)
MAB	Motorized Armour Brigade
MCD	Manchurian Cavalry Division
MPRA	Mongolian People's Revolutionary Army
MRB	Motorised Rifle Brigade
MRD	Motorised Rifle Division
MRR	Motorised Rifle Regiment
P	Platoon
PB	Paratroop Brigade
RBB	Rifle Border Brigade
RC	Reconnaissance Company
RD	Rifle Division
RR	Rifle Regiment
RU	Reconnaissance Unit
TB	Tank Battalion
TBr	Tank Brigade
TR	Tank Regiment (Japanese)
U	Unit

swarmed around us all day long like dark, heavy clouds, and our losses were heavy, all too heavy…" The last two months of the air warfare went by the routine scenario. The 1st Army Group's aviation delivered strikes on Japanese defence sites and protected their troops from the air. Meanwhile, the scarce Japanese bombers would engage in endless futile attempts to deliver their ground troops from the 'noose' – the only result being further costly losses. On August 29 the Soviet summaries reported four Ki-27 and one Ki-30 aircraft destroyed; on August 30, eighteen fighters and two bombers and on August 31 twenty-one fighters and one bomber, admitting the loss of two I-16 fighters. Japanese propaganda, however, adhered to its 'once-and-for-all policy' and exaggerated their claims to forty-six kills. Even if we acknowledge the Japanese command's data authenticity, the Kwantung Army's loss rate amounted to four fighters per day, while Japanese industry could only supply one new Ki-27 fighter every day. These rates imply that the continuation of large-scale combat missions would inevitably result in Japanese fighter stock being quickly exhausted. The casualty rate among expert Japanese pilots should be also taken into consideration. For instance, on August 27 the best IJA fighter pilot H. Sinohara was killed. By then, he was reported to have shot down fifty-eight

⋂ The Japanese pilot H. Sinohara's belongings as removed from his aircraft.

aircraft (though, how many of them were actual kills and how many were just propaganda will never be known). On August 31, Soviet troops swept the enemy back behind the Soviet-claimed state border and began preparations for defensive operations and began construction of two new airfields in the liberated territory. Thus G.K. Zhukov accomplished his mission in Mongolia.

Chapter 5
Cessation of hostilities

For the Japanese, the situation worsened day by day. On August 23 they were, one might say, stabbed in the back by Germany, the principal ally of Japan under the Berlin-Rome-Tokyo tripartite 'Axis' treaty. Berlin, in fact, betrayed Tokyo with the signing a non-aggression pact with USSR, which implied that in the case of the probable full-scale war, Japan would have to fight the Soviets all alone. Meanwhile, the Japanese had already suffered defeat at Lake Khasan in 1938, and were on the edge of suffering a much more painful defeat at Khalkhin Gol. In addition, they were still engaged in their war against Chiang Kai-shek who had unlimited human resources at his disposal. On August 28 the Japanese Cabinet of H. Kutaro resigned having assumed the burden of the defeat and the new Japanese Premier S. Togo and his ministers offered a cessation of hostilities to the USSR. Some combat activities in the air continued, but Soviet bombers were now mostly used for reconnaissance, with the single exception of a large-scale bombing raid on Sugar

⟳ Lieutenant T. Kiroki shot down three Soviet aircraft with his Ki-10 fighter.

Loaf Mountain at Numurun Gol on September 2. Thirty-eight bombers with fighter cover approached the target and level-bombed from 2,000m. The mission was accomplished without casualties. The biggest air combat during the wind-down phase of the conflict took place on September 1 when from the Soviet side, 188 fighters were engaged whereas the Japanese could bring up about 100 fighters. The Soviet pilots claimed twenty kills, their Japanese counterparts – thirty-three. The actual losses appear to include three I-16 and five Ki-27 aircraft. Two Soviet pilots were killed, and one pilot, M. Kulak, captured. On September 2, some Ki-10 'old-timers' appeared in the air for the first time in a mixed group with the Ki-27 fighters. Well, the dogfight's final score was four to one in favor of the Soviets. But – of the four Japanese aircraft shot down three were the newer Ki-27 and only one was the old Ki-10 fighter. On the next day, fifteen I-16s and eleven I-153s encountered seventeen or eighteen Ki-10s and soon another group of twenty-four I-16s arrived, at which point the enemy aircraft fled. Soviet sources reported nine Japanese fighters as shot down and one I-16 and one I-153 lost.

In September 5 seven Ki-10s and a Ki-27 were added to the score and of those, two Ki-10 biplanes went down onto Mongolian troops. In September, Captain Gorlov's squadron of fifteen I-16s arrived bringing the Soviet fighters' ratio further up to four-to-one and as for the bombers, the Red Army already had almost ten times as many aircraft as the Japanese. The IJA air forces ongoing reorganisation resulted in General Giga relinquishing command, and all the air regiments being transferred to the Joint Aviation Command in charge for China, Korea and Manchukuo headed by General E. Ebasi. At this point, all the parties began to wind down the conflict. On September 12, Y.V. Smushkevich was recalled to Moscow along with the group of some two dozen of the best aces. A wing of TB-3 heavy bombers left for the Trans-Baikal Military District for redeployment towards the Polish border. However, the Japanese allowed themselves a final desperate raid against the Soviet airfields and on September 14 they sent ten bombers and forty-five fighters, which were duly met by seventy-five I-16s and fifteen I-153s. Although both

↻ Japanese pilots with a Ki-10 fighter.

sides would later boast to have won, it proved to be a sort of stalemate as not a single aircraft was actually shot down and was in fact a form of 'fighting reconnaissance'. On the next day, about 200 aircraft suddenly attacked Tamtsag Bulak airfield and for the first time the newer Ki-32 bombers of the 45th Regiment participated in a raid. Having seemingly relaxed in anticipation of a ceasefire, the Soviet command lost their concentration and it proved to be a costly oversight. The fighters were taken by surprise and once in the air, they were immediately fired on from above by the Japanese fighters. Soon, dozens of I-16s arrived from the 56th and the 70th IAP and saved the day. Although the Japanese reported thirty-nine kills and the Soviet pilots nineteen, the actual losses were limited to one I-16 and one I-153 fighter on the Soviet side, and nine Japanese fighters and a Ki-32 bomber. Six of the fighters shot down were Ki-27s of the fresh 59th Regiment under Major Y. Kuro's command, and recently withdrawn from Hankow. On the same day of September 15, a tri-partite agreement was signed in Moscow between the Soviet Union, Mongolia and Japan for a cessation of the hostilities at 1:00 pm the following day.

Counting the Cost

From September 16 onwards no air combat actions took place, although Soviet and Japanese fighters loitered alongside their own borders. On September 27, POWs and the bodies of the dead were exchanged.

The Soviet side returned five captive pilots and fifty-five bodies. Japanese sources also indicated that five POWs committed 'hara-kiri' suicide. In the period from May 22 through September 15 1939, Soviet aircraft performed 20,524 sorties, including 14,458 (or more than 70%) in September. Soviet Command estimated the Japanese losses as 646 aircraft and that total included 588 aircraft reported as shot down (including 529 fighters, 42 bombers and seventeen reconnaissance), fifty-eight aircraft reported as destroyed on the ground (thirty-five fighters, two bombers, fifteen reconnaissance and six transports), and fourteen aircraft as shot down by anti-aircraft artillery. The Japanese claimed to have destroyed a total of 1,162 Soviet aircraft in the air and ninety-eight on the ground. From data comparisons drawn from the above and throughout the text the reader can clearly see the propaganda nature of such claims. The Soviet air force detachment in Mongolia hardly could have lost more aircraft than it ever had there. Contemporary Russian historians believe that the Soviet reports overestimated the Japanese losses fourfold, and the Japanese boosted the actual Soviet losses, at least, sixfold. The most effective Soviet fighter pilot was Captain S. Gritsevets, although exact number of his kills was never established. Russian historian N.G. Bodrykhin, however, believes that the Commander of the 70th IAP, Captain N.P. Zherdev was the highest scoring ace with eleven kills. Also worth noting is the 70th regiment's M.P. Noga with

♎ Soviet pilots try out a captured Japanese passenger car.

nine kills and Major S.P. Danilov of 56th IAP and Senior Lieutenant V.G. Rakhov with eight kills each.

Here, we must take into consideration the Red Army Air Force's reporting practice of that period, in that enemy losses were reported on the basis of the pilot's personal statements – no additional evidence was required. Later, during World War II, the casualty statistics would be much more precise requiring a ground observer's confirmation or a special team ordered to examine the crashed aircraft and return with its nameplate or some part with the factory identification mark before the enemy aircraft would be confirmed and reported as actually destroyed. Given the absolutely unrealistic statistics of wins reported by the Japanese, one must suggest the same subjective judgment criteria. The actual losses of Soviet aviation at Khalkhin Gol in the period from 21 May through 15 September amounted to 251 (or 252) aircraft (including 105 I-16, four I-16P, sixty-five I-15bis, twenty-two I-153, fifty-two (or fifty-three) SB, one TB-3 and R-5 planes). The stated total includes forty-three aircraft lost to technical failures or accidents. However, the reported total did not include the aircraft that had been written off during or after the campaign by reason of excessive wear or irreparable damage. We know, however, that 436 aircraft (mostly fighters) were sent to workshops for repair. The figure looks somewhat overblown due to

♎ Senior Lieutenant M.P. Noga of the 70th IAP was the second Soviet ace of the Khalkhin-Gol campaign with nine victories.

the repeated counting of the same aircraft once they were repaired. The air force manpower losses amounted to 174 killed and 113 wounded, including eighty-eight lost in the air.

The Soviet bombardment aviation at Khalkhin Gol was far more active than its Japanese counterpart. The key was their high-speed bomber regiments and during the Khalkhin Gol campaign, these aircraft performed a total of 2,015 air sorties and 74.2% of these were raids on enemy positions. The total losses amounted to fifty-two (or fifty-three) bombers, including the eight lost for non-operational reasons. As for the bombers destroyed by the enemy, thirty-four SBs were shot down in dogfights, ten were shot down by anti-aircraft artillery, and one was hit on ground. The three bomber regiments' total flying personnel losses were reported to be seventy-seven including twenty-three pilots, twenty-five navigators and twenty-nine gunners. However, later, one pilot and one navigator were recovered in a course of postwar exchange of prisoners. Japanese reports do not differentiate their own losses between aircraft shot down and aircraft written-off. A total of 162 was reported as lost, including the two Manchurian civil transports contracted by the IJA. Japanese losses by aircraft types are as follows: one Ki-10, ninety-six Ki-27s, eighteen Ki-30s, six Ki-21s, one BR.20, 15 Ki-4s, 13 Ki-15s, six Ki-36s, one Ki-34, one J (a license Fox Moth), one Typhoon, and two Fokker F-VII/3m). In addition, the Japanese report 220 aircraft repaired after battle damage. Russian historians believe the Japanese statistics to be a deliberate underestimate. For instance, their figures match neither the cumulative total of Japanese reported daily losses nor the data of the on-ground inspection of debris – in particular, a single Ki-10 fighter reported as lost is an especially ridiculous statement. The IJA's air force losses in terms of manpower include 152 killed and sixty-six severely wounded, including casualties amongst ground personnel. The exact losses among the Japanese flying personnel remains unclear as their reports include only the aggregate total of killed and badly wounded: 163 persons. While the Soviet data includes the missing in the total losses, the Japanese reports, apparently, do not. Whether any Japanese pilots were given any awards for the campaign is also ambiguous. In the Soviet Union a special service medal was awarded to all participants, and many pilots received regular wartime orders and medals. Captain S. Gritsevets, Y.V. Smushkevich and G. Kravchenko

⋒ This anonymous Soviet pilot is fully entitled to be happy seeing the two brand-new orders attached to his chest – a Soviet one and a Mongolian one – they were the standard awards for bravery at Khalkhin-Gol.

were awarded their second 'Hero of the Soviet Union' stars and many pilots were also honoured with Mongolian awards. In general, the Khalkhin Gol battles appeared to be a rehearsal, a preparation for similar war that was to be fought on the Pacific coast, and would begin two and a half years later. During the first phase of the combat actions, the Japanese had better equipment and better trained personnel whereas the Soviet empire was often equipped with older aircraft and their pilots lacked combat training and practice. However, as soon as the Soviet Union received their newer fighters and bombers and properly trained aces arrived to pass on their expertise to the others, the situation changed radically. By the end of the conflict, the Japanese could no longer offset their losses, and had to rely on obsolete equipment such as Ki-4 and Ki-10 biplanes, and the Japanese pilots also became overtired and demoralised, a direct result of flying too many missions with too few hours of rest in-between, and they seemed to loose their inherent 'will-to-win spirit'. In that situation, a crushing defeat was the most logical outcome.

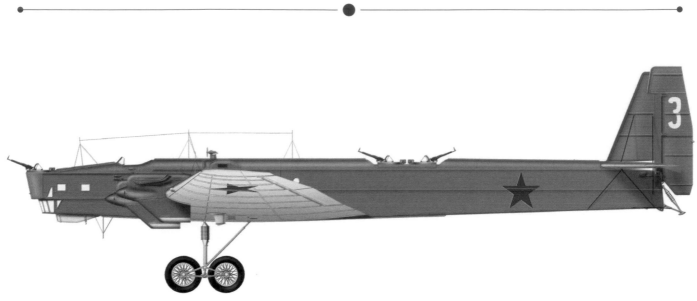

TB-3 4M-17 bomber, 'White 3'

Squadron commanded by Major Egorov. Until around 1937 almost the only type of camouflage for the upper surfaces of Soviet aircraft was green 3B. In order to cover the metal surfaces gloss green AE-7 enamel was used, and this colour slightly changed the shade depending on the time of the year. The lower surfaces are light blue.

R-6, 'White 2', transport aircraft

Upper surfaces are painted in green AE-7 enamel; the lower surfaces are light blue.

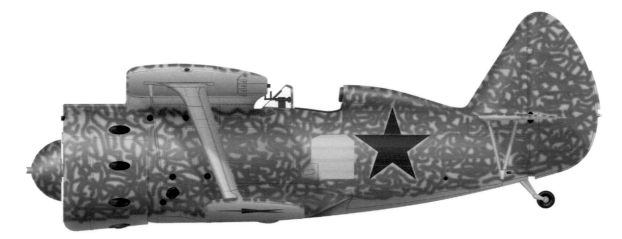

I-153 of the 70th IAP

The aircraft is painted in overall light grey AE-9 enamel (or AE-8 aluminium). The narrow wavy stripes are sprayed on the upper surfaces (most likely using green 3B paint).

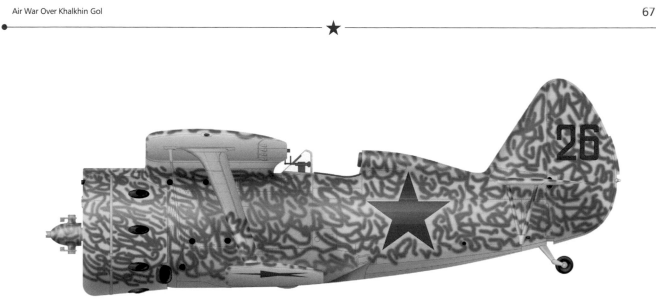

I-153, 'Red 26', of the 70th IAP

Flown by Assistant Squadron Commander, Viktor Gusarov. The aircraft is painted in overall light grey AE-9 enamel (or AE-8 aluminium). The narrow wavy stripes are air brushed on the upper surfaces (most likely using green 3B paint).

I-153, 'Red 29', of the 56th IAP

The aircraft is painted in overall light grey AE-9 enamel (or AE-8 aluminium). Green areas of upper surface camouflage are sprayed most likely using green 3B paint.

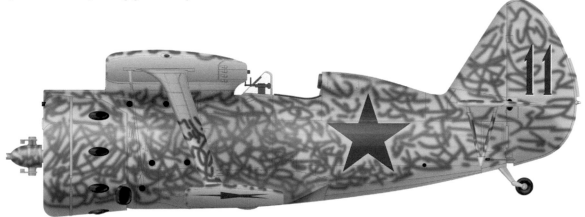

I-153, 'Red 11', of the 22nd IAP

Flown by Commissar V.N. Kalachev, August 1939. The aircraft is painted in overall light grey AE-9 enamel (or AE-8 aluminium). The narrow wavy stripes are air brushed on the upper surfaces (most likely using green 3B paint). Note the white trim on the red tactical number.

Colour views by Andrey Yurgenson

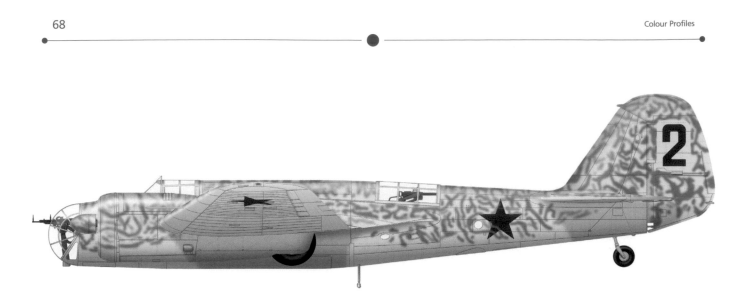

SB 2M-103, 'Red 2', of 28th Special Bomber Regiment

The aircraft is painted in overall light grey AE-9 enamel (or AE-8 aluminium). The narrow wavy stripes are sprayed on the upper surfaces (most likely using green 3B paint).

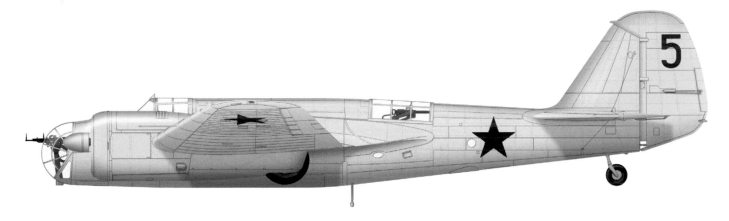

SB 2M-103, 'Red 5'

The aircraft is painted in overall light grey AE-9 enamel (or AE-8 aluminium).

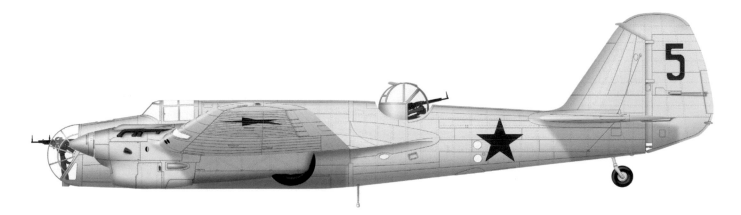

SB 2M-105, 'Red 5', equipped with MV-3 turret

Bain Tumen airfield. The aircraft is painted in overall light grey AE-9 enamel (or AE-8 aluminium).

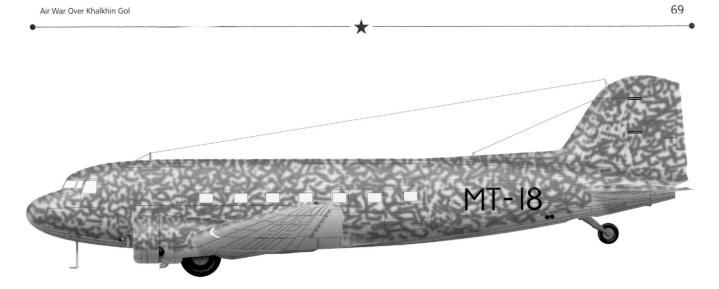

DC-3, 'Black MT-18'

Transport plane which participated in the conflict. The aircraft is painted in overall light grey AE-9 enamel (or AE-8 aluminium). The narrow wavy stripes are sprayed on the upper surfaces (most likely using green 3B paint).

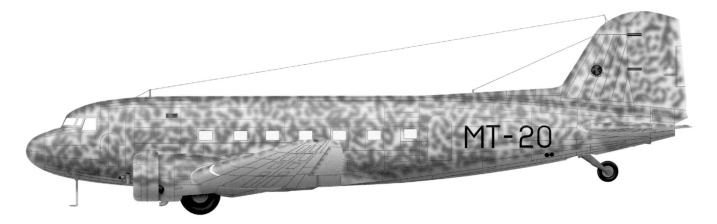

DC-3, 'Black MT-20',

Transport plane which participated in the conflict. The aircraft is painted in overall light grey AE-9 enamel (or AE-8 aluminium). The narrow wavy stripes are air brushed on the upper surfaces (most likely using green 3B paint).

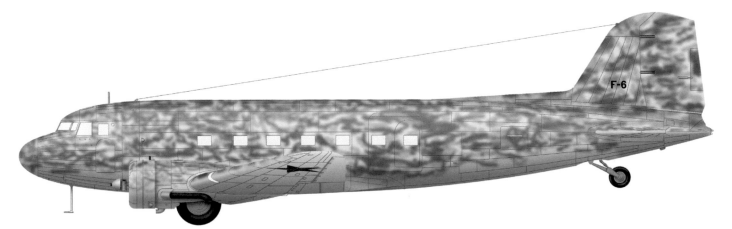

DC-3, 'Black F-6', transport aircraft

The aircraft is painted in overall matt AE-8 aluminium enamel. Green blotches on the upper surfaces were most likely added in the field using 3B paint.

Colour views by Andrey Yurgenson

I-15bis, 'Red 3', of the 3rd Squadron, 70th IAP

This aircraft was lost in an accident near Ulan Bator on 27 April 1939 and flown by Lieutenant Rybakov. The aircraft's upper surfaces are painted in green AE-7 (or 3B) enamel, and the lower surfaces are aluminium AII matt varnish. Note white trim on the tactical number and red/white cap on the tail.

I-15bis, 'Red 14', of the 70th IAP

The upper surfaces are painted in green AE-7 (or 3B) enamel, and the lower surfaces are aluminium AII matt varnish. Note white trim on the tactical number and red/white cap of the tail.
The red stars also have black trim.

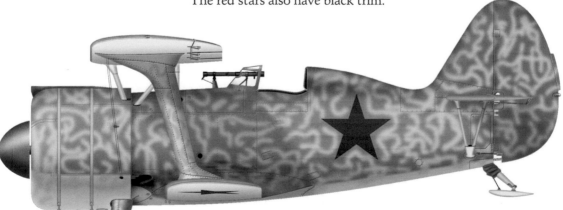

I-15bis

The upper surfaces are painted in green AE-7 (or 3B) enamel, and the lower surfaces are blue-grey. The narrow wavy stripes are sprayed on the upper surfaces using aluminium or light grey AII matt varnish.

I-16 Type 5, 'Red 4'

The upper surfaces are painted in green AE-7 (or 3B) enamel, and the lower surfaces are blue-grey. Note white trim on the tactical number and absence of red stars on the fuselage.

I-16 Type 5

The upper surfaces are painted in green AE-7 (or 3B) enamel, and the lower surfaces are blue-grey. Note the repositioning of the red star from the fuselage to the tail.

I-16 Type 10, 'White 2', of the 70th IAP

Tamtsag Bulak airfield, July 1939. The upper surfaces are painted in green AE-7 (or 3B) enamel, and the lower surfaces are blue-grey. Note red cap and white identification stripe on the tail.

Colour views by Andrey Yurgenson

I-16 Type 10, 'White 3', of the 70th IAP. July 1939

The aircraft is painted in overall light grey AE-9 enamel (or AE-8 aluminium). The green areas on the upper surfaces were added 'in service' and over the factory-applied paint, most likely using 3B.

I-16P 'White 5 1' of the 22nd IAP

Flown by Junior Lieutenant Katalov. The upper surfaces are painted in green AE-7 (or 3B) enamel, and the lower surfaces are blue-grey. Note different size tactical numbers and white identification stripe around the upper part of the fuselage.

I-16 'Red 5, yellow 7', Type 10

The upper surfaces are painted in green AE-7 (or 3B) enamel, and the lower surfaces are blue-grey. Note different colour and size of the tactical numbers. Spinner and rudder tip are yellow.

Colour views by Andrey Yurgenson

I-16 Type 10, 'White 5', of the 70th IAP. July 1939

The aircraft is painted in overall light grey AE-9 enamel (or AE-8 aluminium). Green areas on the upper surfaces were added 'in service' and over the factory-applied paint, most likely using 3B.

I-16 Type 10 of the 22nd IAP

Flown by Junior Lieutenant Davidenko. The upper surfaces are painted in green AE-7 (or 3B) enamel, and the lower surfaces are blue-grey. Note blue-grey quick identification stripe and absence of red stars on the fuselage. White identifications stripes were added around the wingtips.

I-16 Type 10 of the 22nd IAP

The upper surfaces are painted in green AE-7 (or 3B) enamel, and the lower surfaces are blue-grey. Note blue-grey quick identification stripe and absence of red stars on the fuselage.

Colour views by Andrey Yurgenson

I-16 Type 10, Arutoki airfield, Western Manchuria, May 1939

The plane was tested at Tachikawa. The aircraft is painted in overall light grey AE-9 enamel (or AE-8 aluminium). Red stars and tactical numbers are painted over with a Japanese light grey colour, which had a slightly different shade. Red Hinomaru's were added to the wing.

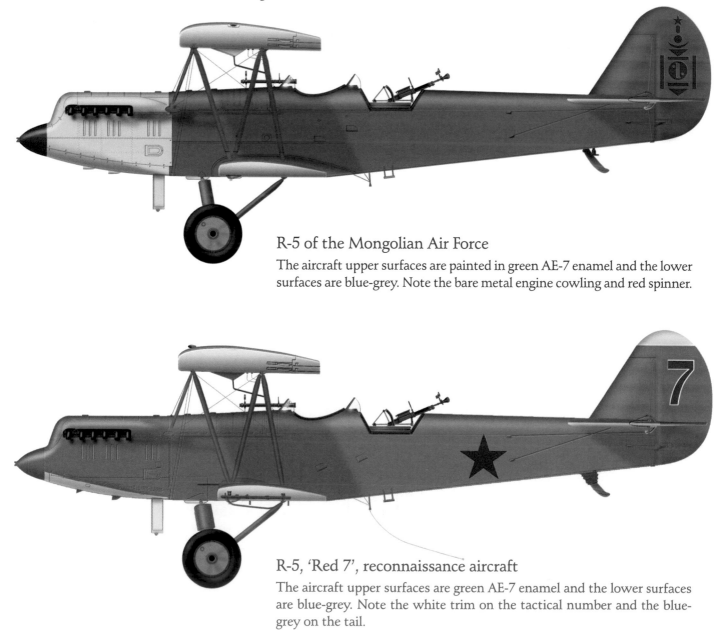

R-5 of the Mongolian Air Force

The aircraft upper surfaces are painted in green AE-7 enamel and the lower surfaces are blue-grey. Note the bare metal engine cowling and red spinner.

R-5, 'Red 7', reconnaissance aircraft

The aircraft upper surfaces are green AE-7 enamel and the lower surfaces are blue-grey. Note the white trim on the tactical number and the blue-grey on the tail.

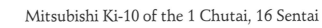

Mitsubishi Ki-10 of the 1 Chutai, 16 Sentai

The aircraft is painted in overall light grey. Note the white identification stripes on the tail.

Mitsubishi Ki-10 of the 2 Chutai, 10 Hiko Sentai

The upper surfaces of the wing and tail, as well as the complete fuselage and landing gear spats are camouflaged in brown and olive green. This is the so-called 'Kumogata' camouflage. The lower surfaces of the wing and tail are light grey. Note the white identification stripes on the tail.

Mitsubishi Ki-10 of the 10 Sentai.

The upper surfaces are camouflaged in brown and olive green. The lower surfaces are painted in light grey. Note the white identification stripes on the tail.

Colour views by Andrey Yurgenson

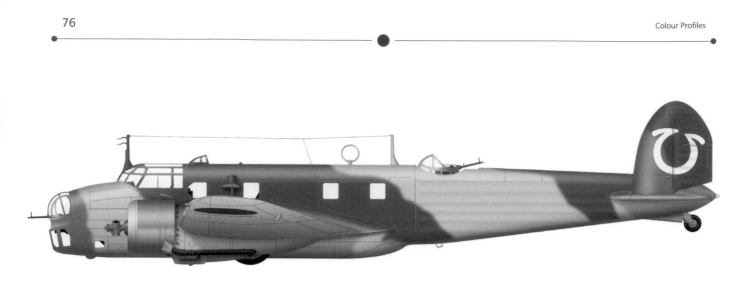

Fiat BR.20 of the 12 Sentai. June 1939

Upper surfaces are camouflaged in the areas of yellow, brown and green colours. Lower surfaces are grey.

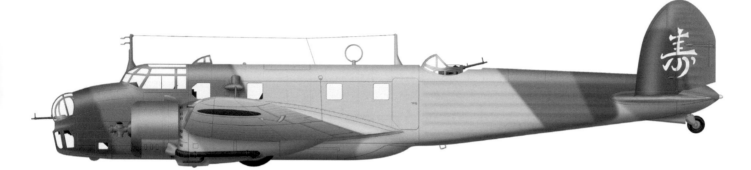

Fiat BR.20 of the 12 Sentai. June 1939

In the second half of the 1930s the Italian Air Force developed a series of camouflage colours (Mimetica). The colours were applied in wide wavy stripes. Iinitially, only the wing upper surfaces were camouflaged, but then the fuselage was covered as well. The initial colours used were yellow (Giallo Mimetico). green (Verde Mimetico), and brown (Marrone Mimetico), although these shades may differ between manufacturers. Four types of yellow are known to have been used – Giallo Mimetico 1, 2, 3, and 4; three types of green – Verde Mimetico 1, 2, and 3; and three variations of brown – Marrone Mimetico 1 and 2, and dark brown Bruno Mimetico. In addition to the above, the shades Marrone Mimetico 53193 and Verde Mimetico 53192 were extensively used. The lower surfaces were painted in grey Grigio Mimetico, which was the standard colour for Italian aircraft till 1941.

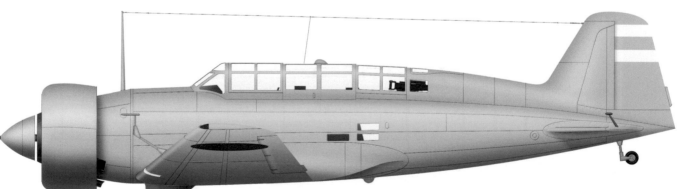

Mitsubishi Ki-10-I of the 1 Chutai, 15 Sentai

The aircraft is painted in overall light grey. Note two white stripes on the rudder. The all-metal aircraft of army aviation were painted in a gloss grey-green colour. The carrier based aircraft were painted in J1 (ash-grey). The fabric-covered control surfaces were painted in gloss grey-green on army aircraft and in aluminium powder mixed with varnish on naval aircraft.

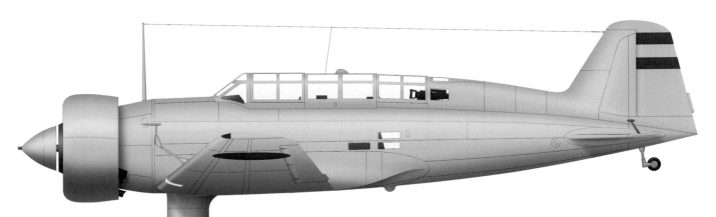

Mitsubishi Ki-10-I of the 2 Chutai, 15 Sentai

The aircraft is painted in overall light grey. Note the two red stripes on the rudder.

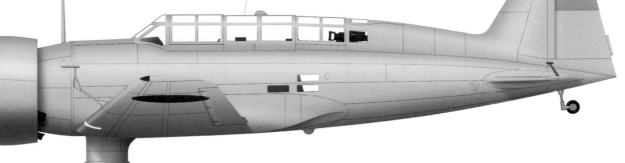
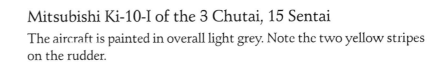

Mitsubishi Ki-10-I of the 3 Chutai, 15 Sentai

The aircraft is painted in overall light grey. Note the two yellow stripes on the rudder.

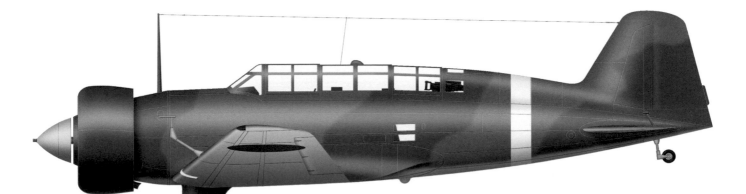

Mitsubishi Ki-10-I of the 10 Sentai

The aircraft was painted in overall light grey. Then the upper surfaces have been camouflaged with green and brown areas. Note white identification stripe around the rear part of the fuselage.

Colour views by Andrey Yurgenson

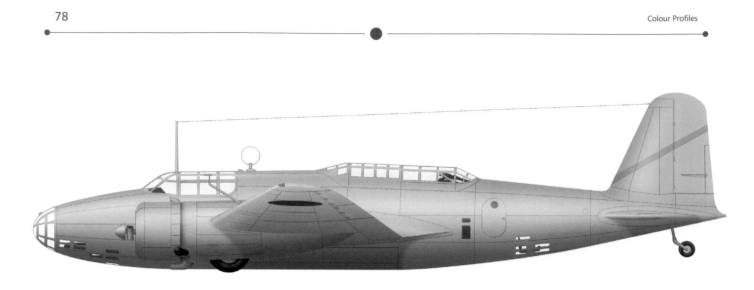

Mitsubishi Ki-21-I-Ko of the 1 Chutai, 61 Sentai

The aircraft is painted in overall light grey. Note yellow identification stripe across the tail.

Mitsubishi Ki-21-I-Ko of the 2 Chutai, 61 Sentai

The aircraft is painted in overall light grey. Note blue identification stripe across the tail.

Mitsubishi Ki-21-I-Ko of the 3 Chutai, 61 Sentai

The aircraft is painted in overall light grey. Note red identification stripe across the tail.

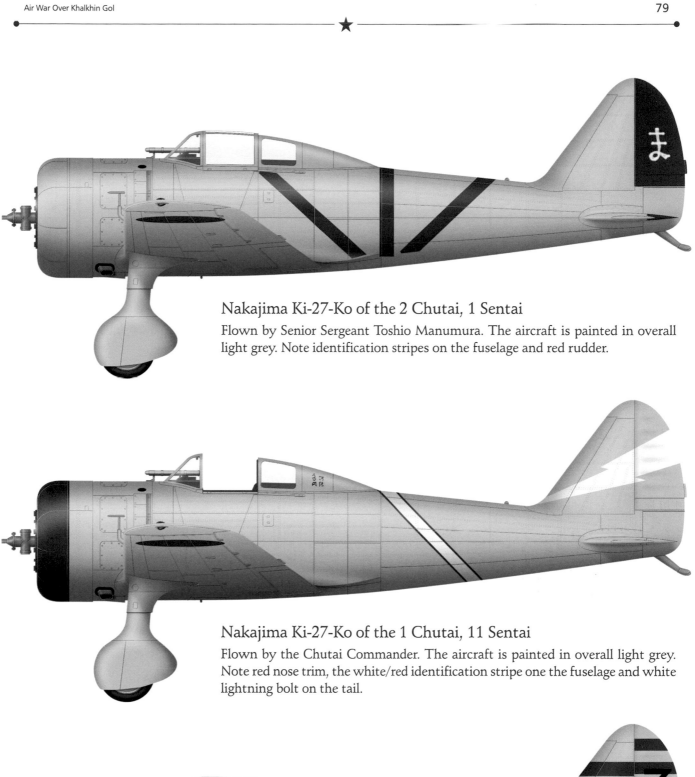

Nakajima Ki-27-Ko of the 2 Chutai, 1 Sentai

Flown by Senior Sergeant Toshio Manumura. The aircraft is painted in overall light grey. Note identification stripes on the fuselage and red rudder.

Nakajima Ki-27-Ko of the 1 Chutai, 11 Sentai

Flown by the Chutai Commander. The aircraft is painted in overall light grey. Note red nose trim, the white/red identification stripe one the fuselage and white lightning bolt on the tail.

Nakajima Ki-27-Ko of the 2 Chutai, 24 Sentai

Flown by Senior Sergeant Goro Nishiro. August 1939. The aircraft is painted in overall light grey. Note identification stripes on the fuselage and tail.

Colour views by Andrey Yurgenson

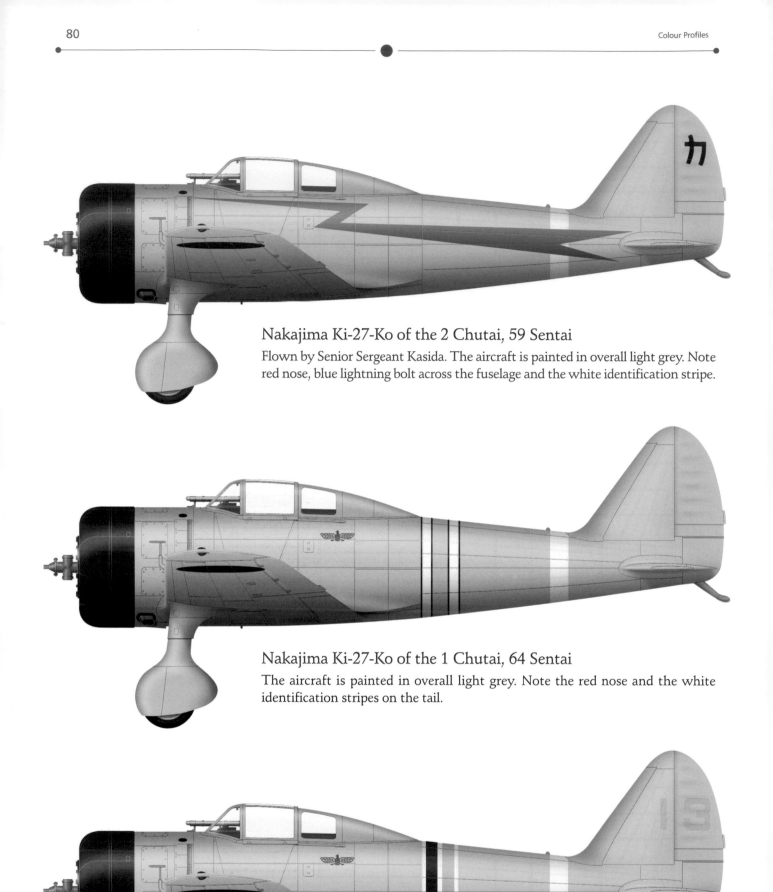

Nakajima Ki-27-Ko of the 2 Chutai, 59 Sentai

Flown by Senior Sergeant Kasida. The aircraft is painted in overall light grey. Note red nose, blue lightning bolt across the fuselage and the white identification stripe.

Nakajima Ki-27-Ko of the 1 Chutai, 64 Sentai

The aircraft is painted in overall light grey. Note the red nose and the white identification stripes on the tail.

Nakajima Ki-27-Ko, 'Yellow 13', of the 1 Chutai, 64 Sentai

Flown by Lieutenant Hiroshi Sekiguchi. The aircraft is painted in overall light grey. Note the red nose and the identification stripes on the tail.

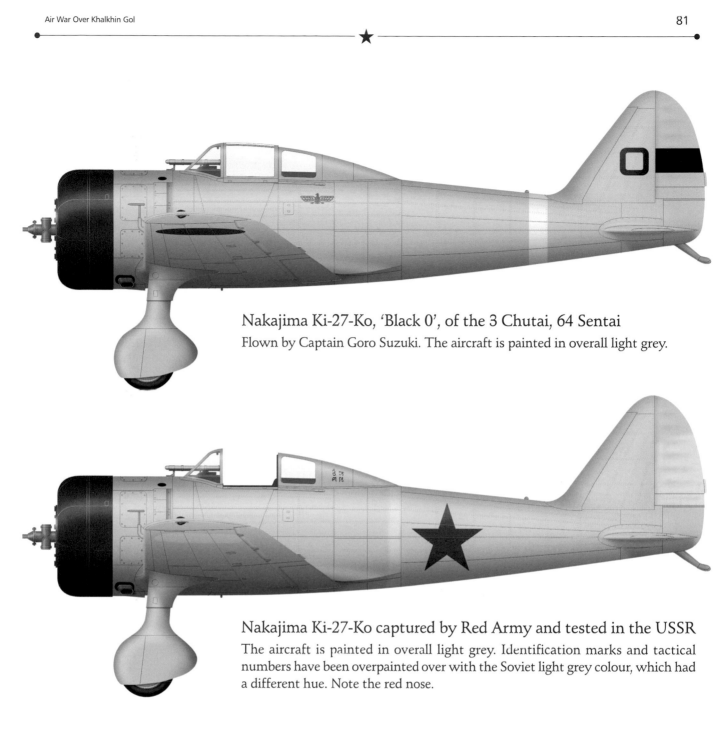

Nakajima Ki-27-Ko, 'Black 0', of the 3 Chutai, 64 Sentai
Flown by Captain Goro Suzuki. The aircraft is painted in overall light grey.

Nakajima Ki-27-Ko captured by Red Army and tested in the USSR
The aircraft is painted in overall light grey. Identification marks and tactical numbers have been overpainted over with the Soviet light grey colour, which had a different hue. Note the red nose.

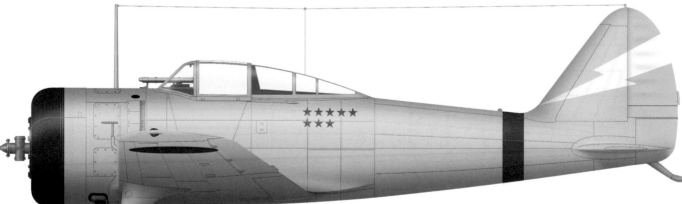

Nakajima Ki-27-Otsu of the 1 Chutai, 11 Sentai
Flown by Captain Kenji Simada. June 1939. The aircraft is painted in overall light grey. Note the red nose and the identification stripe around the tail. Victory markings are painted as small red stars under the cockpit.

Colour views by Andrey Yurgenson

Nakajima Ki-27-Otsu

Flown by Warrant Officer Hiromisi Sinohara. The aircraft is painted in overall light grey. Note red wheel spats, and the white identification stripe and lightning bolt on the tail. Victory markings are painted as small red stars under the cockpit.

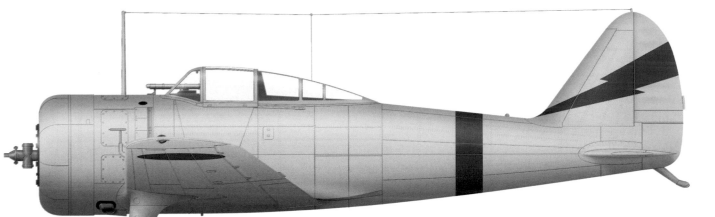

Nakajima Ki-27-Otsu of the 2 Chutai, 11 Sentai

The aircraft is painted in overall light grey. Note the red identification stripe and the lightning bolt on the tail.

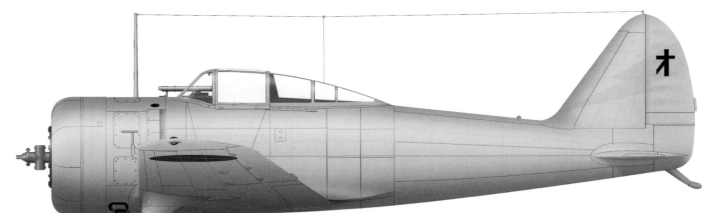

Nakajima Ki-27-Otsu of the 3 Chutai, 11 Sentai

Flown by Sergeant Zenzaburo Otsuka. September 1939. The aircraft is painted in overall light grey. Note the yellow lightning bolt on the tail.

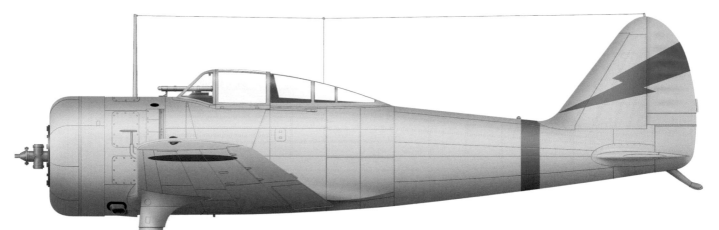

Nakajima Ki-27-Otsu of the 4 Chutai, 11 Sentai

Flown by Captain Jiyozo Ivanisi. The aircraft is painted in overall light grey. Note the green identification stripe and lightning bolt on the tail.

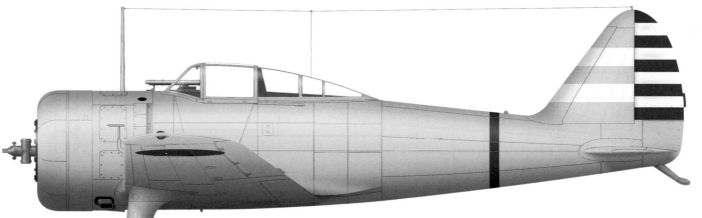

Nakajima Ki-27-Otsu of the 1 Chutai, 24 Sentai

Flown by the Chutai Commander. The aircraft is painted in overall light grey. Note the white and red identification stripes on the tail.

Colour views by Andrey Yurgenson

Russian
Polikarpov I-15bis
Fighter

This single-seat fighter was developed in 1937 by the Central Design Bureau under the leadership of Nikolay Polikarpov and was based on the design of the earlier I-15 fighter, but introduced considerable changes. Although having a mix of construction materials, this aircraft was mostly fabric-covered both on the fuselage and wings, and in contrast to the I-15, the upper wing did not have the prominent 'gull' shape. The cockpit was open with a windshield, and the fixed, non-retractable main landing gear was fitted with wheels in the summer and skis in winter. The aircraft was

★ I-15bis	
Upper Wingspan (m)	10.2
Length (m)	6.27
Weight empty (kg)	1,310
Weight take-off (kg)	1,730
Max speed at ground level (km/h)	327
Max speed in flight (km/h)	379
Service ceiling (m)	9,300
Range (km)	520

↻ A Soviet pilot posing near an I-15bis.

⋂ I-15bis of the 1938 series in standard colours, with the lower part of the engine cowling and the wheel spats painted in matt silver-grey.

powered by an M-25V 775hp radial engine, which was a modified version of the Wright SCR-1820-F3 Cyclone, built under licence by Factory No. 19 in Perm. The engine powered a two-blade metal fixed-pitch propeller and armament included four 7.62-mm PV-1 machine guns with bomb racks under the lower wing. The pilot's seat was fitted with an armour back plate. The I-15bis was produced at Moscow Factory No.1 from the end of 1937 till the end of 1939 with a total of 2,408 aircraft being built. In service, the fighter was considered as reliable and relatively easy to fly and quite adequate for the average pilot's skills. From 1938, I-15bis fighters were used by Soviet and Chinese pilots in air combat against the Japanese over China and in the same year the type was successfully used in the conflict near Lake Khasan, where it undertook light ground-attack duties. At the onset of the Nomonhan conflict, these aircraft were being gradually transferred to ground-attack roles and were used as both fighters and ground-attack aircraft.

⋂ I-15bis.

Russian
Polikarpov I-16
Fighter

The I-16 fighter was developed by the Central Design Bureau under the leadership of Nikolay Polikarpov in 1933-34 and the type was originally designated as TsKB-12 and one of the first of the 'new wave' of cantilever wing monoplane aircraft with retractable landing gear, and an enclosed cockpit. However, this Polikarpov design was not all-metal, as the monocoque fuselage was constructed of glued veneer sheets, whilst the wing and empennage structures were metal. The wing was covered with plywood and fabric, and as with all Soviet fighters of the time, the aircraft flew with skis in winter and wheels in summer. Series production of the I-16 was started in the middle of 1934 at Factory No. 34 in Moscow, and in 1935 by Factory No.21 in Gorkiy which soon become the primary site for I-16

★ I-16 Type 18	
Wingspan (m)	9.0
Length (m)	6.04
Weight empty (kg)	1,428
Weight take-off (kg)	1,830
Max speed at ground level (km/h)	411
Max speed in flight (km/h)	464
Service ceiling (m)	9,470
Range (km)	485

production. In 1937 Factory No.153 in Novosibirsk also began production with a total of 9,540 aircraft being produced – a record for the prewar period. By the middle of 1939, the I-16 underwent several stages of modernisation. The first aircraft were 'Type 4' and

⊕ Soviet pilots near an I-16 Type 10.

I-16 Type 5 c/n 123954, produced by Moscow Factory No. 39, 1934

‹› Tests of the first I-153 M-25V prototype took place in September 1938.

powered by the 480hp M-22 engine (the licensed copy of the French Gnome-Rhone 9A Jupiter engine built at Factory No.29 in Zaporozhye). The 'Type 4' had an enclosed cockpit (the canopy could be opened by moving it forward), a two-blade metal fixed-pitch propeller, and two 7.62-mm ShKAS machine guns, which had a higher firing rate than the earlier PV-1. The 'Type 4' was considered as a temporary measure, being mostly for training purposes. The first truly combat version of the I-16 was the 'Type 5' powered by an M-25 engine. The other features of the aircraft remained unchanged, while external differences included a smaller engine cowling diameter and blunt-shape propeller spinner. The I-16 was developed as high-speed agile fighter, and its compact size allowed it to perform more extreme manoeuvres, however, this resulted in an extremely high sensitivity to the deflection of the control surfaces. Thus having such a small stability margin, the aircraft required constant action from the pilot and demanded high professional skills, for example when firing its machine guns, the aircraft had a tendency to swing which resulted in a high dispersion of bullets. In 1937 the factories began production of the Type 10 version, which had a strengthened airframe, improved M-25V engine and more powerful armament with four ShKAS machine guns. This type featured an open cockpit with the

elongated fixed windshield, as the enclosed canopy was much criticised by pilots due to the poor field of vision.

The Type 10 was the basis for the Type 17 (also designated as I-16P, where P stood for Pushechniy (cannon-armed), which had two ShKAS machine guns replaced with 20-mm ShVAK cannon; the second pair of ShKASs in the fuselage as well as the bomb-carrying capability were retained. In addition to the long-barrel cannon, the aircraft sported a tail wheel replacing the skid. The cannon armament allowed the fighter to attack enemy aircraft from greater ranges and it could also be used as a light non-armoured ground-attack aircraft. The most numerous version used during the Nomonhan conflict was the I-16 'Type 18' powered by an 1,100hp M-62 engine with two-blade variable-pitch VISh-6A propeller. The conflict also saw the use of a small batch of specially modified I-16s, able to fire 82-mm RS-82 rocket projectiles and these aircraft featured a metal skin on their lower wing surfaces in the area of the guide rail attachments. Each aircraft was capable of carrying eight RS-82s. Later on the I-16 was built in other variants which were fitted with the more powerful M-63 engine, an improved armament of cannon and high-calibre machine guns and additional external fuel tanks, as well as an uprated bomb-carrying capacity of 500lb.

Soviet
Polikarpov I-153
Fighter

Nikolay Polikarpov was a staunch supporter of the 'two-fighters' theory, believing that the Air Force needed both high-speed monoplanes and manoeuvrable biplanes. Continuing the line begun by the I-15 and I-15bis, Polikarpov developed the I-153 designation which returned to the 'gull-wing' configuration. The first production aircraft built for service trials were powered by the M-25V engine, but later the fighter received a new 1,100hp M-62 with a two-speed supercharger and twin-blade variable-pitch

★ I-153 with M-62 engine	
Upper wingspan (m)	10.0
Length (m)	6.17
Weight empty (kg)	1,348
Weight take-off (kg)	1,765
Max speed at ground level (km/h)	364
Max speed in flight (km/h)	424
Service ceiling (m)	10,700
Range (km)	560

metal AV-1 propeller. The landing gear was retractable, with wheels in summer and skis in winter and the aircraft was armed with four 7.62-mm ShKAS machine guns and could carry a 200lb bomb load or jettisonable 50 or 100 litre fuel tanks. The I-153 was in series production at Factory No.1 in Moscow from the beginning of 1939 till the end of 1941. In total 3,437 fighters of this type were built. In the Nomonhan conflict early series fighter were used with maintenance provided by the production factory teams, who rectified any defects. Uprated versions of the I-153 were built, powered by M-63 engines and with improved armament, including the BS high-calibre machine guns.

∩ I-153 on the Mongolian steppes, summer 1939.

⊂ A pair of I-153's in flight.

Russian
Polikarpov R-5
Reconnaissance Aircraft

The R-5 was developed as long-range reconnaissance aircraft by the Department of Land-Based Airplanes Central Design Bureau under the leadership of Nikolay Polikarpov in 1927. It had a mixed construction of wood (pine) as its main material, which was inexpensive and technologically simple. The skin was made of plywood and fabric, while metal panels were used only in the front part of the fuselage. The R-5 used a fixed undercarriage (wheels in summer and skis in winter) and had an open cockpit for two crew members. The aircraft was powered by a 680hp or 730hp BMW VI engine, later on replaced by the Soviet M-17, M-17B, or M-17F driving a wooden two-blade fixed-pitch propeller. The 300kg bomb load was carried externally, and armament included one

★ R-5	
Upper wingspan (m)	15.35
Length (m)	10.56
Height (m)	3.6
Weight empty (kg)	2,108
Weight normal take-off (kg)	2,730
Weight max take-off (kg)	3,350
Maximal speed at the ground (km/h)	210
Maximal speed in flight (km/h)	229
Cruise speed (km/h)	175
Service ceiling (m)	6,400
Range (km)	960
Range with additional fuel tanks (km)	1,450

↻ Restored R-5 at Russian Air Force Museum in Monino.

↻ Soviet pilot posing near R-5 biplane.

♁ R-5 crews discuss the coming mission.

synchronized PV-1 machine gun positioned under the engine cowling, and two DA machine guns in the rear turret. These aircraft were also exported to Iran and fitted with 1924-type Lewis machine guns in the turret, while the front-firing PV-1 was replaced by a Vickers machine gun.

Aircraft series production began in April 1930 at Factory No.1 in Moscow and in August 1931, a batch of five aircraft was assembled at Factory No. 31 in Taganrog, while the production rate at the Moscow-based factory was being gradually increased. In 1934 the R-5 underwent some modernization with new landing gear and wheel brakes, an M-17F engine, and an improved bomb load. The type was built as a both a short- and long-range reconnaissance aircraft (for the latter fitted with additional fuel tanks), a light bomber (800kg) and ground-attack aircraft. In the latter version (R-5Sh, LSh-5 or ShR-5) it was equipped with additional bomb racks for carrying up to 40 small-calibre bombs and four PV-1 machine guns in the fairings under the lower wing. The rear cabin was

fitted with a single DA machine gun and special versions were developed as well – the R-5T torpedo bomber and the float equipped R-5a reconnaissance aircraft. R-5 production was ended in 1935 with a total of 5,030 aircraft produced, not including the SSS (3S) ground-attack aircraft, which in fact was another specialised version of the R-5. In the middle of the 1930s the R-5 was the most numerous aircraft in Red Army Air Force service and participated in combat operations against rebels in Middle Asia, on the Mongolia-Manchurian border in 1936, and also fought in the Spanish Civil War and in the conflict near Lake Khasan. In Mongolia, the R-5 and R-5Sh were in service with both Soviet and Mongolian aviation, and the First Air Force used them for liaison and transportation purposes, while the Second Air Force used them in the night bombing role. As a transport aircraft, the R-5 could transport two or three passengers or cargo in the rear cabin.

Russian
Tupolev SB
High-Speed Bomber

The SB high-speed bomber was developed as a response to American Martin 139 bomber, and the task of producing a new counter-type was given to the Central Aero and Hydrodynamic Institute headed by Andrey Tupolev with design work carried out by a team under the leadership of Aleksander Arkhangelskiy. Fighting for speed, Tupolev went much further than the Martin designers as he not only used the two-engined cantilever wing monoplane layout with retractable undercarriage and enclosed cockpits, but also critically minimised the frontal area in order to decrease aerodynamic drag. Initially the bomber was designed for use with Cyclone engines, but later French 750hp Hispano-Suiza 12Ybrs power plants were used under the M-100 designation and built at the Rybinsk factory. The SB was an all-metal monoplane with retractable undercarriage and a crew of three, and the M-100 engines were fitted with front honeycomb radiators

★ SB with M-100 engines	
Wingspan (m)	20.33
Length (m)	12.4
Height (m)	4.775
Weight normal take-off (kg)	5,732
Weight max take off (kg)	6,462
Max speed at ground level(km/h)	325
Max speed in flight (km/h)	423
Effective ceiling (m)	9,560
Range (km)	1,500

and two-blade, fixed-pitch metal propellers. Armament included four 7.62-mm ShKAS machine guns – two in the nose at the navigator's station, one in a Tur-9 turret in the rear cabin and one in a belly hatch for firing aft. A full bomb load of 600kg was accommodated inside the bomb bay. SB series production began in February 1936 at Factory No.22 in Moscow and was followed in 1937 at Factory No.

↻ An emergency landing made by an SB 2M-103 with three-blade propellers. Note the typical spotted camouflage used in the Khalkhin Gol area.

⋂ SB 2M-103 of the 96th series, produced in 1939, and in service with an aviation unit of the Moscow Military District, and seen here on the taxiway of NII VVS airfield.

125 in Irkutsk. The bomber was built in different versions until 1941, and a total of 6,831 was manufactured.

Aircraft deliveries to the Red Army Air Force units started in May 1936, in November it was used in the Spanish Civil War, in October 1937 it saw in combat in China against the Japanese, and in 1938 at Lake Khasan. The aircraft underwent numerous modifications. In October 1936, more powerful 860hp M-100A engines were fitted, in May 1937 three-blade variable pitch VISh-2 propellers based on the licensed Hamilton airscrews were added and a retractable ski undercarriage and cylindrical cartridges for small calibre bombs, so-called 'Onisko Buckets', were applied. The most significant change was undertaken in 1938 on the 'conditional 96th series' where the internal bomb capacity was increased from 600 to 800kg, and two external bomb racks were added raising the total bomb load to 1,500kg. The external carriers could also

↻ SB 2M-103 of the 96th series carrying an external bomb load.

☉ An emergency landing being executed by an SB. Note the two-blade propellers without spinners.

accommodate discharge devices for chemical agents or two additional 368 litre fuel tanks. The pneumo-hydraulic landing gear was replaced with electro-hydraulic, and this was also used for flap extension. The aircraft was powered now by 960hp M-103 engines and the trailing aerial was replaced with a fixed example.

In fact, the complete set of improvements was introduced from the 101st series at the Moscow-based factory and these were fitted with M-100AU engines which had a longer service life. In 1939, the factories began installing new upper MV-3 and lower MV-2 turrets on the SB, and there are photos showing such aircraft in Mongolia. The Nomonhan conflict saw the use of several different versions of the SB, built by different factories in different years, and in order to unify the fleet within a given regiment or squadron, the command tried to put together the aircraft built by the same factory, or nearest production series.

Russian
Tupolev TB-3
Heavy Bomber

The four-engined TB-3 was originally planned carrying heavy outsize cargo on external attachments, however, the specification was later changed in favour of using the type as a day and night bomber. The aircraft was developed at the Central Aero and Hydrodynamic Institute headed by Andrey Tupolev in 1927–29 and had a cantilever wing with a tube and section construction, covered by a non-structural corrugated metal skin. The fixed undercarriage was originally fitted with large single wheels which were later replaced by two-wheel tandem bogies. The pilot's

⭐ TB-3 with M-17 engines	
Wingspan (m)	39.5
Length (m)	24.4
Weight empty (kg)	11,207
Weight take-off (kg)	17,050
Max speed at ground level (km/h)	198
Service ceiling (m)	3,800
Range (km)	1,350

cockpit was open and the aircraft powered by German BMW VI V-engines which were introduced into series production under licence at the Rybinsk factory under the M-17 designation. The engines were fitted with two-blade wooden fixed-pitch propellers. Originally, the aircraft carried a crew of twelve, but this was later reduced to eight. Armament included eight 7.62-mm DA machine guns – six of which were paired and mounted in three turrets (one in the front and two in the back), while other two were single-mounted in retractable underwing B-2 mounts nicknamed 'Pants'. 100kg bombs were placed inside the bomb bays in containers, while heavier 2,000kg bombs were carried externally.

In the transport role, the TB-3 could carry up to twelve paratroopers inside the fuselage and various other

⋂ TB-3s in flight over Amur river.

⋃ TB-3 powered by M-17 engines.

⟳ TB-3s sit ready.

equipment such as cars and trucks, armoured vehicles, guns and light tanks in an external rack, mounted between the main landing gear. Production began in February 1932 at Factory No.22 in Moscow, and another Moscow-based factory No.39 also began manufacturing in November same year. At the end of 1934 Factory No.18 in Voronezh was also building the TB-3, but only five aircraft were made there. TB-3 series production ceased at the end of 1938, with a total of 819 built. In the course of production, the type underwent several modifications. The M-17 engines were replaced with the improved M-17B, and with the M-17F. TB-3 heavy bombers were introduced into service in April 1932, and their first combat use was at the end of 1937 in China, while in August 1938 they also made bomb strikes on Japanese and Manchurian troops near Lake Khasan.

⟳ TB-3s flying in a three-aircraft formation.

Japanese
Mitsubishi Ki-15
(Army Type 97) Reconnaissance Aircraft

The Ki-15 was the first specialised Japanese long-range reconnaissance aircraft, and designed by Mitsubishi under the leadership of F. Kono, T. Kubo and S. Midzumo in 1935. The Ki-15 was an all-metal, cantilever wing monoplane and in order to improve its aerodynamic characteristics, the skin was made of smooth aluminium panels with counter-sunk rivets, with only the rudder being fabric-covered. The undercarriage was fixed and provided with spats and the aircraft carried a crew of two. Power was provided by a 750hp Ha.8 radial engine which drove a two-blade fixed-pitch metal propeller, and its defensive armament included one 7.69-mm Type 89 machine gun fitted on a rotatable mount in the rear cabin. Ki-15 series production began in May 1937 at the Mitsubishi factory in Nagoya and continued until the beginning of 1941 with a total of 489 aircraft being built, including the C5M version for the Navy. Units of the Japanese Imperial Army Aviation received the first of this new reconnaissance aircraft in summer 1937 and its high speed and good flying characteristics resulted in only small losses. Several versions of the Ki-15 were designed, but only one – the Ki-15-I (R-97, according to the Soviet designation system), saw operation in Nomonhan.

● Ki-15-I	
Wingspan (m)	12.0
Length (m)	8.49
Height (m)	3.24
Weight empty (kg)	1.399
Weight normal take-off (kg)	2,033
Weight max take off (kg)	2,300
Max speed (km/h)	480
Cruise speed (km/h)	320
Service ceiling (m)	11,400
Range (km)	2,400

⊙ Ki-15 reconnaissance plane.

⊙ Ki-15 which crash landed near Blagoveshchensk in 1940.

Japanese
Nakajima Ki-4
(Army Type 94) Reconnaissance Aircraft

In 1933 the Nakajima Company received an order for the development of light reconnaissance aircraft which could also be used for close air support. The project's chief designer Shigejiro Ohwada, chose a layout with an elliptical shaped upper wing and monocoque fuselage, which used the Type 91 fighter as its inspiration. The aircraft was powered by a 640hp Ha.8 radial engine driving a two-blade variable-pitch metal propeller, and the crew of two was accommodated in open cockpits. The aircraft was armed with three or four 7.69-mm Type 89 machine guns – two fixed forward-firing and another one or two in the rear cabin. Production began in July 1934 at the Nakajima factory in Ota and the first version was the Ki-4-Ko with wheel spats, and the later series were equipped with underwing bomb racks. The Ki-4-Otsu version, which was built from 1937 mostly at the Tachikawa and Manshu factories had an engine exhaust collector instead of the individual exhaust pipes, and was fitted with bomb racks under the wing. The later series used low-pressure tyres without spats. Production ceased in February 1939, with a total of

● Ki-4	
Upper wingspan (m)	12.0
Length (m)	7.73
Height (m)	3.5
Weight empty (kg)	1,664
Weight take-off (kg)	2,474
Maximal speed in flight (km/h)	284
Service ceiling (m)	8,000

516 aircraft produced. Japanese Imperial Army Aviation began to use the Ki-4 in 1935 and the type took an active part in the initial stages of the Japan-China conflict. The Soviet designation system defined the Ki-4 as the LB-94, treating it as a light bomber rather than a reconnaissance aircraft.

⋃ Ki-4 reconnaissance planes in the field.

Japanese
Mitsubishi Ki-21
(Army Type 97) Bomber

The Ki-21 belonged to the same generation of bomber aircraft as the Soviet SB, and its development was carried out using the same concept. It was an all-metal twin-engined monoplane with smooth skin, enclosed cabins and retractable undercarriage and was developed by the Mitsubishi Company under the leadership of engineers Nakata and Ozawa in 1936. The Ki-21 was slightly larger and heavier than the SB,

● Ki-21-Ia	
Wingspan (m)	22.5
Length (m)	16.0
Height (m)	4.35
Weight empty (kg)	4,691
Weight normal take-off (kg)	7,492
Weight max take-off (kg)	7,916
Maximal speed in flight (km/h)	432
Service ceiling (m)	8,600
Normal range (km)	1,500
Max range (km)	2,700

but used the 1,080hp Ha.6-II engines and three-blade variable-pitch metal propellers. The bomber was armed with three 7.69-mm Type 89 machine guns, one mounted in the nose and two in the upper and lower parts of the rear cockpit. Normal bomb load was 750kg, maximum 1,200kg. Production began in 1937 at the Mitsubishi factory in Nagoya, and when production ceased in September 1944, a total of 2,064 aircraft had been produced. From August 1938 Ki-21s were used as bombers and long-range reconnaissance aircraft and during the Nomonhan conflict, Ki-21-Ia (Ki-21-I-Ko) aircraft were transferred to the combat area. This type was designated as the SB-97 in Soviet quick-recognition manuals.

↷ Ki-21 bombing-up.

↶ Ki-21 bomber.

♠ Ki-21 bomber.

♠ Ki-21 on a bombing mission.

Japanese
Fiat BR.20
(Type I) Bomber

The two-engined BR.20 Cicogna bomber was created in 1935 by the Italian aircraft manufacturer Fiat under the leadership of Celestino Rosatelli and was a cantilever-wing monoplane with retractable undercarriage, enclosed cockpits and twin tails. The fuselage was const ructed with a welded steel tubular frame with a metal-covered front part and fabric-covered rear. The wing was also partially fabric-covered, while the control surfaces had a complete fabric skin. The aircraft was powered by two Fiat A.80 RC.20 radial air-cooled 1,000hp engines and its defensive armament included three 12.7-mm Breda-SAFAT machine guns in the nose, upper turrets, and a lower mount, and it had a bomb load of some 1,000kg. Production began in September 1936 at the Aeritalia factory in Turin, which produced a total of 580 bombers by the end of 1943, including a number of civil BR.20A and BR.20L versions. The bomber entered service with the Regia Aeronautica in February 1937, and was used in the Spanish Civil War by the Italian Legionary Air Force. In 1937, during their visit to Italy, the Japanese representatives were shown Ca 135 and CR.20 bombers, and placed an order for 100 of the latter type – with payment being made by delivery of soya beans from Manchuria. The bombers began to arrive in Japan at the beginning of 1938, and were introduced into

BR.20	
Wingspan (m)	21.56
Length (m)	16.75
Height (m)	4.3
Weight empty (kg)	6,500
Weight take-off max (kg)	10,100
Max speed (km/h)	430
Cruise speed (km/h)	350
Service ceiling without bombs (m)	7,200
Range (km)	2,000

service in March under the Type I designation. Some sources indicate that the aircraft were delivered without armament and the standard 7.69-mm Type 89 machine guns were installed in Japan. In fact, Italy managed to ship only seventy-five aircraft as the Japanese government refused the remainder of the order. Also in 1938 the Fiats were sent to the front in China, from where they were transferred to Mongolia, and although they were present in the Nomonhan conflict they were relegated to second line duties and replaced Ki-21 bombers.

↻ Fiat BR.20 bomber of Japanese Air Force at Chinese airfield.

Japanese
Mitsubishi Ki-30
(Army Type 97) Bomber

The Ki-30 was developed under the same specification as the Ki-32, however, the Mitsubishi designers, headed by Kawano, Ohki and Mizuno, selected a compact 960hp Ha.6 two-row radial air-cooled engine. The bomber turned out to be smaller and lighter than the Ki-32, featuring the same bomb load and armament. The Ki-30 was an all-metal cantilever-wing monoplane with enclosed cockpit for two crew members, a fixed spat-covered undercarriage, and a bomb load of 300 to max 450kg was accommodated inside the fuselage. Armament included two 7.69-mm Type 89 machine guns – one in the wing panel, and the other at the gunner/radio operator's station in the rear cockpit. Production began at the Mitsubishi factory in Nagoya in March 1938, and also at the 1st Arsenal of Army Aviation in Tachikawa. When production ceased in 1940 at Nagoya 618 aircraft

● Ki-30	
Wingspan (m)	14.55
Length (m)	10.34
Height (m)	3.645
Weight empty (kg)	2,230
Weight normal take-off (kg)	3,332
Max speed (km/h)	432
Cruise speed (km/h)	380
Service ceiling (m)	8,570
Range (km)	1,700
Max range (km)	1,960

had been produced and by 1941 Tachikawa had produced some sixty-eight models. Ki-30 light bombers were used in combat in China in 1938 and Soviet sources designated the type as the LB-97.

⮎ Ki-30 on a combat mission over China.

⮌ Ki-30 light bomber, designated by Soviet sources as LB-97

Japanese
Kawasaki Ki-32
(Army Type 98) Bomber

The Ki-32 was a 'new generation' light bomber type, which was to replace Japan's older biplanes. The aircraft was developed by the Kawasaki Company under the leadership of Isamu Imashi and Shiro Ota in 1936–37 and was an all-metal monoplane with a cantilever mid-mounted wing. The two crewmen were seated in the enclosed cockpit and the aircraft had a fixed undercarriage provided with spats. To power the aircraft, the designers selected 950hp Ha.9-II liquid-cooled Vee engine driving a three-bladed metal propeller. The bomb load was carried inside the fuselage and the armament included two 7.69-mm Type 89 machine guns – one fixed in the front, and the other in a turret in the rear cockpit. Series production began in July 1938 at the Kawasaki factory in Akashi and some 846 examples were produced up to 1940. Compared to another similar light bomber, the Ki-30, the Ki-32 had a slower speed, but a greater service ceiling and was more manoeuvrable. It was also believed that its liquid-cooled engine made it more vulnerable in combat. Prior to the Nomonhan conflict the Ki-32 was briefly in service at the front in China and Soviet sources designated the type as the LB-98.

● Ki-32	
Wingspan (m)	15.0
Length (m)	11.64
Height (m)	2.9
Weight empty (kg)	2,349
Weight normal take-off (kg)	3,539
Weight max take-off (kg)	3,762
Max speed (km/h)	423
Cruise speed (km/h)	300
Service ceiling (m)	8,920
Normal range (km)	1,960
Max range (km)	1,960

↻ Flight of Ki-32s in 1938.

↻ A Ki-32 light bomber, designated by Soviet sources as LB-98

⋒ Japanese flight crew in the rear cockpit of the Ki-32.

⋒ Ki-32 light bomber.

Japanese
Nakajima Ki-27
(Army Type 97) Fighter

The Ki-27 was the first Japanese monoplane fighter and was developed by the Nakajima Company in 1935–36 under the leadership of Koyama Yasushi. It was an all-metal cantilever, low-mounted wing monoplane with a fabric skin covering only the control surfaces. To power the aircraft, the designers selected the 650hp Ha.1a (Ha.1-Ko) engine with a two-blade metal propeller. Armament included two 7.69-mm Type 89 synchronized machine guns mounted inside the fuselage. This aircraft also won the competition against the Ki-28 and Ki-33 fighters. Production began in June 1937 at the Nakajima factory in Ota, and initially the Ki-27-Ia (Ki-27-Ko) version was built, powered by a 780hp Ha.1b (Ha.1-Otsu) engine, and featured an open cockpit. All aircraft were fitted with radio receivers, whilst every third aircraft had a transmitter. The following version was the Ki-27-Ib (Ki-27-Otsu), which had a modified oil cooler, a fully enclosed cockpit and also this version removed the fuselage upper fairing. In addition, a camera gun and four bomb carriers, for 25kg bombs each, were installed. From 1938 the Ki-27 was also in production at the Mansu factory in Harbin, in Manchuria and in total, both factories built some 3,399 aircraft, not counting the two-seater Ki-79 training version. Around 2,000 Ki-27s were built in Ota. The Ki-27 was successfully used in combat in China in 1938 and during the Nomonhan conflict, both Ki-27 versions (Ko and Otsu) were in service. The Soviet sources designated the type as the I-97.

Ki-27	
Wingspan (m)	11.31
Length (m)	7.53
Height (m)	3.25
Weight empty (kg)	1,110
Weight normal take-off (kg)	1,547
Weight max take-off (kg)	1,790
Max speed (km/h)	470
Cruise speed (km/h)	350
Service ceiling (m)	10,040
Normal range (km)	625
Max range (km)	1,710

Ↄ Ki-27 fighter of the 1st Regiment.

Ↄ A Ki-27-Otsu.

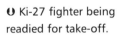 Ki-27 fighter of the 1st Squadron of 64th Regiment in flight over China.

⊃ A Ki-27 fighter of the 59th Regiment.

↻ Ki-27 fighter being readied for take-off.

Japanese
Kawasaki Ki-10
(Army Type 95) Fighter

The Ki-10 fighter was developed by the Kawasaki Company under the leadership of Takeo Doi in 1934 and was a typical biplane fighter of the time, and was intended for short-range air combat. The aircraft featured an all-metal design with fabric covered wings, fixed undercarriage with its pilot seated in an open cockpit. The aircraft was powered by an 850hp Ha.9-II-Ko liquid-cooled Vee engine, which was a modified licenced copy of the German BMW IX driving a two-blade (on prototypes) or three-blade (on series aircraft) fixed-pitch propeller, and its armament included two 7.69-mm Type 89 machine guns. Production of the Ki-10 began at the Kawasaki factory in Akashi in December 1935 and by October 1937, when production ceased, 300 aircraft had been built. From the 185th aircraft, the Ki-10-II was produced and featured an increased wing span and elongated fuselage. Ki-10 fighters were used in China in 1937 and

● Ki-10-II	
Upper wingspan (m)	10.02
Length (m)	7.55
Height (m)	3.0
Weight empty (kg)	1,360
Weight take-off (kg)	1,740 *
Max speed (km/h)	400 *
Service ceiling (m)	11,500
Range (km)	1,100

* NII VVS data for captured aircraft gives:
  Weight take-off (kg) 1,883 and Max speed (km) 377

one captured Ki-10 was transported to the Soviet Union, repaired and tested at the Air Force Scientific Research Institute. Soviet sources designated this aircraft as the I-95. By the time of the beginning of hostilities on the Mongolian border, the Ki-10 was considered an outdated aircraft.

↻ Captured Ki-10 fighter during tests at NII VVS.

Combat Strengths & Losses

★ The 57th Special Corps (1st Army Group) Air Force Composition

Type	21/06/39	01/07/39	01/08/39	17/08/39	20/08/39
I-15bis	56	45	57	57	62
I-16	95	93	194	495	244
I-153	–	–	70	41	70
SB	135	132	181	187	181
TB-3	–	–	23	22	23
R-5	15	10	7	7	7
Total	301	280	532	809	587

Note: Includes the attached Mongolian Squadron aircraft stock. Only operational aircraft are included.

● Japanese Aviation in the Conflict Area

Type	16/06/36
Ki-27	78
Ki-10	–
Ki-30	6
Ki-32	–
Ki-21	12
BR.20	12
Ki-15	12
Ki-4	–
Ki-36	6
Total	126

★ Soviet and Mongolian Aviation Losses at Khalkhin Gol

Type	Combat	Non-combat	Total
I-16	83	22	105
I-16P (type 17)	4	–	4
I-15bis	60	5	65
I-153	16	6	22
SB	44	8	52
TB-3	–	1	1
Total	207	42	249

● Japanese and Manchurian Aviation Losses at Khalkhin Gol (official Japanese data)

Type	Lost	Irreparably Damaged	Total
Ki-10	1	-	1
Ki-27	62	34	96
Ki-30	11	7	18
Ki-21	-	-	-
BR-20	-	1	1
Ki-4	1	14	15
Ki-15	7	6	13
Ki-36	3	3	6
KKJ	-	1	1
Bf 108 *	-	1	1
Fokker F-VII/3m *	-	3	3
Total	85	70	155

* Civil Manchurian aircraft

Index

¶ references a picture
§ references a colour profile
¤ references a table

♠ Fiat BR.20 bomber.

ᕡ Ki-30 light bomber in flight.

Maps